The Cycle of Time

Ancient Knowledge, India
and Uncovered Secrets

Simone Boger

The Cycle of Time – English version
Copyright © 2014 Simone Boger
All rights reserved

All rights reserved. No part of this book may be reproduced in any manner without written permission, except for quotations embodied in critical articles or reviews.

Proofreading : Ashton Playsted
Cover Design: Fena Lee

Website: www.cycleoftime.com

ISBN-13: 978-1499624915
ISBN-10: 1499624913

Contents

Preface to the New Edition 5

Introduction 9
    The Question of Time 15
    The Question of Being 18
    The Mechanism of Consciousness 21
    Karma 22
    Swastika 25
    Home 27

Sat Yuga 33
    Bharat 38

Treta Yuga 45
    The Expansion of the Kingdom 47
    The Fall 49
    The Beginning of Memory 54

Dwapur Yuga 59
    Beginning Once Again 61
    Bhakti ~ Paths of Devotion 65
    Kala - The Spirit in the Art 69
    Ancient Deities 74
    In the Attempt of Reconnecting 77
    Castes 78
    The Four Stages of Life 80
    Creation is a mystery: Ko Veda? 81

Kali Yuga 87
- India – the Night of Brahma 88
- The Decline of Bhakti 90
- Science 92
- The Science of the Psyche 93
- In Search of an Origin 95
- The System 99
- The Mahabharat 101
- Arjuna 107
- The Need for Silence 108

Sangam Yuga 113
- The Divine Play 116
- Shiva Nataraja 119
- Ancient Raja Yoga 122
- Waves of Change 124

Preface to the New Edition

The cyclic view of history is a complete and integrated model of reality that was the basis of ancient philosophical thought for millennia before it was relegated to oblivion. During the Renaissance, the discovery and translation of lost texts brought back this knowledge of the cycle of ages, even if only to a small circle of initiates.

Plato and Aristotle, and later Leonardo da Vinci and Giordano Bruno, along with many others, shared this worldview. Later, a few English Romantic poets were inspired by the same vision. According to Percy Shelley, "History is a cyclic poem written by time upon the memories of man."

The movements that tried to bridge Eastern and Western metaphysics had their source in the legacy of the ancients, especially in the spiritual traditions of India and Egypt. In India, the understanding of the eternal cycle was never completely lost, even though it branched into a number of different approaches. The basic concepts, however, remained contained within the very fabric of life and thought and in the spiritual beliefs of the people.

I grew up reading esoteric books and often found references to arcane and mysterious texts. This is how I was confronted very early by two versions of history: the linear and evolutionist version I learned in school, and the forgotten history—the one that spoke of gods and the Fall, of higher dimensions and lost knowledge. My head used to spin with these mysteries, leading me to consider taking up archaeology.

However, it took me no more than a few classes to realize that I would not be able to spend my life pondering over fragments of ruins. Intuitively I sensed that whatever I was searching for was not to be found in academia. A few years later, this knowledge came to me in the most unexpected way, almost as a gift. And instead of a scattered jigsaw puzzle, a complete picture appeared, even if initially it was only in its most basic form. This was my starting point in learning about a perspective of history that provides an understanding of our individual, spiritual story as deeply connected to external events. Exploring this correspondence over time triggered a huge transformation in my thoughts and actions.

This book was written a few years later, in 1991, with a feeling of gratitude and reverence for the sacred. It contains the essence of the teachings of Raja Yoga and is filled with images and texts that were part of my studies at that time.

Today the cyclic view of history has appeared in other contexts; it is no longer the exclusive property of mystics and yogis. Still, inner stability and mental silence continue to be the means for understanding and assimilating its deeper aspects.

We've been hearing a lot lately about the Maya calendar and other models based on the precession of the equinoxes, which ancient civilizations used to mark the ages. It is in the field of cosmology, however, that the cyclic view is reemerging with the greatest force. Initially restricted to specialized publications, the subject has now entered mainstream media as an alternative to the Big Bang theory.

The cyclic perspective is being revised and is considered by some theorists to be a model that explains unsolved scientific paradoxes. In this theory, the universe's clock has no beginning or end but is nonetheless finite and recurring. Issues involving gravitational singularities—hypothesized locations where gravity and heat become infinite and the laws of physics break down—disappear. In the words of one theorist, it is as if "events are always diverging or evolving away from a potential singularity." The philosophical implications of this view are still more fascinating.

We live in an amazing time when the secrets of the natural world and the dimensions beyond are rapidly being unveiled. Despite crises and uncertainties, the cyclic vision suggests we have reached a point of transition.

The cycle is nothing but the history of the human soul and its journey through life and death, birth and rebirth. It is also the story of our connection with the Source—with God as the Supreme Alchemist. It is his presence and energy that transforms iron into gold, eternally inspiring and perfecting human consciousness and in this way renewing life itself.

Island of Santa Catarina – October, 2008

First English Edition – June 2014

"If the universe may be conceived as a definite quantity of energy, as a definite number of centres of energy,— and every other concept remains indefinite and therefore useless—it follows therefrom that the universe must go through a calculable number of combinations in the great game of chance which constitutes its existence. In infinity, at some moment or the other, every possible combination must once have been realized; not only this, but it must have been realized an infinite number of times. And inasmuch as between every one of these combinations and its next recurrence every other possible combination would necessarily have been undergone, and since every one of these combinations would determine the whole series in the same order, a circular movement of absolutely identical series is thus demonstrated: the universe is thus shown to be a circular movement which has already repeated itself an infinite number of times, and which plays its game for all eternity...

...Would you have a name for this world; a solution of all your riddles? Do you also want a light, you, most concealed, strongest and most undaunted men of the blackest midnight?"

— *The Will to Power - Eternal Recurrence*
  - Friedrich Nietzsche

Introduction

Shrouded in a kaleidoscope of images, information, and new inventions, we might have been at the threshold of manipulating life according to our will, were we not so distant in responding to so many existential questions. Having created hundreds of philosophies and lived through many ideologies, we might have been at the threshold of a new era, if only we had a reliable reference for our origins and felt certain about what the future holds.

We have been reaching farther and farther boundaries of space, delving deep into the quantum world and wondering how to address the disorder we've created in nature. And yet we know so little about ourselves. What is the real "self"? What is our story? Where do we really come from? Is there a place or an ultimate state we will eventually return to?

India was once a fertile soil for this kind of investigation, and its thinkers made use of a rather interesting analogy for situating man on the path of life. Existence used to be perceived as an unlimited "Cosmic Drama," a play in which man had the role of weaving the threads of history.

This real-life play—*Prabhu Ki Lila*—was never seen as random and chaotic, but as a perfect plot with a plan.

Those who were able to understand the course of history were believed to have realized the purpose of life, as if they were able to "see" how civilizations, religions, and ideologies had risen and declined, letting truths and facts become apparent in constant coherent patterns.

Realizing a wider reality has always been an aim of seekers of self-knowledge. Today we rarely pursue things that can take us to the depth of understanding and wisdom we once possessed. By no means do we hold a truly wide or complete view of history. We have moved away from subtle and deep thought; we have lost the ability to live in close contact with our core.

The turn of the twentieth century has seen the recycling of ancient theories and ideas, and this quest for knowledge has become the foundation for a renaissance of philosophical and spiritual thought and an expansion of science.

But the task of putting this unlimited puzzle together, of tracking the origins of what we call history, has so far not been accomplished. In the days when man contemplated the nature of the Supreme, this last frontier was considered to be in the domain of a super-consciousness.

Scientists and spiritualists will certainly agree on how difficult it is to deal with the absolute. Still, we keep on moving, defining patterns in the fields of neurobiology and mathematics, in physics and astrophysics, seeing the wonder in the intricate structures of fractals.

Even though a complete picture of "reality" still eludes us, there is no reason to doubt that we are getting closer to a complete comprehension of the processes of the universe.

It definitely seems to be an order, even if it is only partially understood.

Yet it is beyond physical form and sound, beyond the reach of science's devices, within the sphere of the invisible that ultimate reality remains hidden.

Finding the "generator principle" or "first cause" seems to be the key to this ancient enigma. This is a riddle believed to be solved at the end of every cosmic cycle, when history would take a new turn.

All great traditions of the past speak of the quest for wisdom, the need to understand that make us so unique and special in creation. These traditions also remind us how the "light" of understanding has always emerged from the depths of darkness, as if knowing and forgetting is but a part of the play. This is probably why it is remembered that "...in the beginning there was the Word."

Swastikas are found everywhere in India. They are on the walls and frescos of temples, on the streets and in the pages of accounting books, in the hands of uncountable gods and goddesses.

Considered an auspicious sign, it portrays the flow of time. It also symbolizes the journey of the soul, revealed at the transition of a cosmic cycle through knowledge—*gyan*—and meditation—*yoga*. Those who get to know the secrets of the cycle are said to become *trikaldarshis*—knowers of the past, present, and future.

The vision of a line following a curve into the distance delineates a world history with no beginning or end. This is how the ancients understood what we call eternity.

An essay on India's soul, whose wisdom once knew no limits, and whose time points almost to midnight now.

Whatever name we may put to the psychic background, the fact remains that our consciousness is influenced by it to the highest degree, and all the more so the less we are conscious of it. The layman can hardly conceive how much his inclinations, moods, and decisions are influenced by the dark forces of his psyche, and how dangerous or helpful they may be in shaping his destiny. Our cerebral consciousness is like an actor who has forgotten that he is playing a role. But when the play comes to an end, he must remember his own subjective reality, for he can no longer continue to live as Julius Caesar or as Othello, but only as himself, from whom he has become estranged by a momentary sleight of consciousness. He must know once again that he was merely a figure on the stage who was playing a piece by Shakespeare, and that there was a producer as well as a director in the background who, as always, will have something very important to say about his acting.

— On the Reeducation of the Germans - Carl Jung

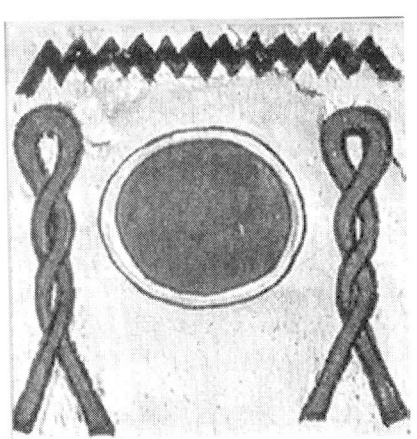

The Question of Time

Modern civilization seems to be pushed by a constant impulse to move forward, at each step trying to overcome former achievements and use its energy to trigger the next discovery or creation. The main thing is movement, production: that which lies ahead. Even when the past is being recycled, things are usually labelled original. Forgetfulness is a human trait. The disappearance of the past contributes to the emphasis on the present and on propelling us forward unquestioningly.

This worldview has been amplified by science, where a fixed idea of linear and evolutionary time has played a part in burying our origins.

Besides the passage of time, our past has also been fragmented by ingenious minds that, at all times and under different circumstances, have been working to maintain the *status quo*. It has been left to historians to try to put the pieces together and assemble the real picture. Yet even they are not free from the burden of their time, and therefore from the influence of an established ideology, whatever it may be.

As we look back into the not-so-very-remote past, we find a completely different perspective of history. *Hum so, so hum*—that which I was, I shall be again—goes an Indian saying. The civilizations of the East, of Egypt and Greece, as well as those of the Pre-Columbian Americans all had a cyclic approach to history. Plato believed that "the same views have arisen among men in cycles, not only once, nor twice, not even a couple of times, but endless times..." and Aristotle thought that all arts and sciences have reached perfection many times in history and later been almost entirely forgotten before being completely lost as a result of global catastrophes.

Just as in nature, where things are consumed and renovated in definite cycles, time—in all its vastness and complexity—follows a rhythm, like a cosmic clock in a movement of eternal recurrence.

In reality, this view of history is still unknown. It throws us back into a glorious past, totally in opposition to an unrealistic journey from a stone age. It identifies us as the descendants of dignified and elevated ancestors, true gods and goddesses who once lived on this very earth. It shows us that within a continual pattern of events, we find civilizations successively ascending and descending and thus making way for new civilizations, which will ultimately cause the events that will once again take us to the point at which everything "started."

Cyclic time is placed within a wider context of life because it is based on the inner journey of the spirit throughout history. It is a metaphysical approach, where the new meets the old and subjective considerations are taken into account.

The more we understand it, the more we rediscover the wisdom and vision of the ancients, which considered man in his totality, in interaction with the material universe and a superior force.

In no other place than India has the issue of existence occupied so many hearts and minds for so long. India is the oldest continuous civilization on the planet, where even today one can still witness passionate discussions over complex and controversial spiritual matters. The way of being and living here was shaped by a permanent force of devotion. Indeed, many aspects of Indian culture have developed from metaphysical or spiritual foundations.

Over time, the many methods of inquiry developed into several schools of thought. Of these, the teachings of Raja Yoga of the Brahma Kumaris have been chosen as the basis of this book.

This perspective concerns both the understanding and the journey of the human soul, also giving us a general idea of the cosmogony and richness of this ancient culture.

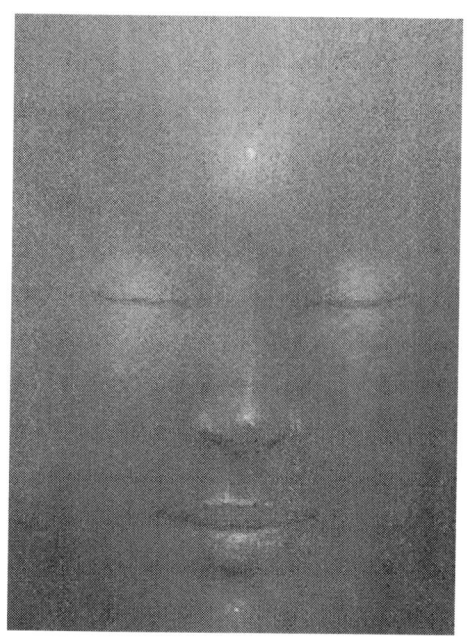

The Question of Being

The psyche is at the core of human history; it is the thread that weaves the plot. It is the human soul that "turns the wheel of time" as it passes through a cycle of lives, of births and rebirths.

Realizing the self as spirit requires deep inner experiences. Meditation is a tool through which we can access and realize our true nature and gradually become aware of and learn to master our innermost self.

Gentle introspection and subtlety of mind are the means of leading us back to our original self—the tiny point of light residing deep inside the brain. As most of us know, there is no known dimension or mathematical formula that could possibly be used to physically measure the soul. To realize the self, one needs depth and a quiet mind.

Through the practice of meditation, our thoughts—the energy flow that carries messages—become focused. We begin to realize that we can consciously choose the feelings we want to express. Experimenting with the source of thoughts results in a clear awareness of who we are and how we function in the world. It is the soul that gives life to the body; the soul is the self.

The Sanskrit word *atma* describes this subtle being as the generator of ideas, emotions, and reasoning that commands its existence through the mechanism of thought. The soul is the life force that makes use of a number of bodies during its journey through history.

> *As a man puts off his worn clothes and puts on other new ones, so the embodied soul puts off worn-out bodies and goes to others that are new. Weapons do not cleave it, fire does not burn it, waters do not wet it, winds do not dry it. For the soul there is never birth or death.*
> *Nor, having once been, does it ever cease to be.*
> *It is unborn, eternal and primeval and it is not slain when the body is slain.*
>
> *– Bhagavad Gita II - 20-23*

Each soul carries its own personality traits and tendencies accumulated and manifested in the course of its lives. Certainly we are all similar in our ways of operating, but we still possess a set of traits that makes us unique individuals. Mind, intellect, and the subconscious are faculties of the soul, used to play our part in the external world.

The human spirit exists eternally and is subject to natural laws, playing the game of life in this ever-changing field of action.

According to the cyclic approach, there is a connection between one's inherent qualities and the moment the soul first descends into or is incarnated in this world. Every soul's life cycle is said to be related to its latent attributes and qualities—its "celestial degrees." Inner potential determines one's first birth at a certain moment in history. From then on the soul is continually reborn in the cycle of *samsara*.

* * *

> *Every soul comes into this world strengthened by the victories or weakened by the defeats of its previous life. Its place in this world as a vessel appointed to honor or dishonor is determined by its previous merits or demerits. Its work in this world determines its place in the world which is to follow this.*
>
> *— The First Principles - Origen*

It is clear that our knowledge and values determine the quality of our thoughts and actions. Our actions, in turn, generate the energy that preordains many aspects of our lives. It is important to understand that on a spiritual level we are never immune to the consequences of our actions.

The soul has an extremely sophisticated mechanism of recording its memories. The Sanskrit word *sanskaras* can be translated as the records, habits, and tendencies that form the roots of our personality.

The observation and mastery of the inner self is a life-long process that can clarify how each external circumstance relates to aspects of inner experience. Tendencies or *sanskaras* are responsible for defining the body, place, and circumstances of birth of every soul.

The Mechanism of Consciousness

A thought emerges from a self-generated movement that causes a deliberation. Before any word or action, there is a thought or intention in the mind, even when we are not conscious of it. Every action is recorded in the subconscious mind, creating impressions—*sanskaras*—in the vast container of one's personal history.

These impressions will once again lead to impulses of realization as they emerge on the surface of the mind. The intellect is able to analyze them, deciding either to initiate or to stop an action; again, this is in accordance with existing tendencies. If a thought is put into action, a new *sanskara* is recorded or an old one is reinforced (habit). These tendencies constantly manifest themselves as intentions or desires to be fulfilled.

In this way, the mind—in the form of ideas, desires, or thoughts—allows whatever memory it recorded in the past to reemerge and is able to acknowledge and recognize things. Recognition generally occurs through external stimuli like words, colors, sounds, and people. The intellect can understand these sensory phenomena and experience them.

#

> *"No man can attain freedom from activity by refraining from action; nor can he reach perfection by merely refusing to act. He cannot even for a moment remain really inactive, for the qualities of nature will compel him to act whether he wants it or not... Therefore do your duty perfectly, without care for the results; for he who does his duty disinterestedly attains the Supreme."*
>
> *– Bhagavad Gita III/4, 5, 20*

Karma—from the Sanskrit *karam*—simply means action. In a spiritual sense, it also indicates the reaction implicit in every action we perform. Our deeds build up into a chain of cause and effect, which in its totality forms a cyclic continuum.

Karma is therefore the energy flow released by the soul in the form of thoughts, words, and actions. As in physics, every action is thought of as an applied force that generates a reaction of equal intensity. In the spiritual field, however, *karma* has the addition of a value. This value is what gives a spiritual dimension to *karma*; it is also what determines the boundary between "good" and "evil." Ethical or moral value is inherent in the law of *karma*.

Karmic residue in the subconscious—our *sanskaras*—builds up inner tendencies, habits, and character traits. These are personality determinants and directly influence the way we think and do things.

The cycle of life can also be seen as a stage on which all of us—real life actors—determine our destiny through the quality of our actions. The more we investigate the philosophy of *karma*, the more we come to understand how free will and predetermination move the wheel of time and how nothing truly happens by chance.

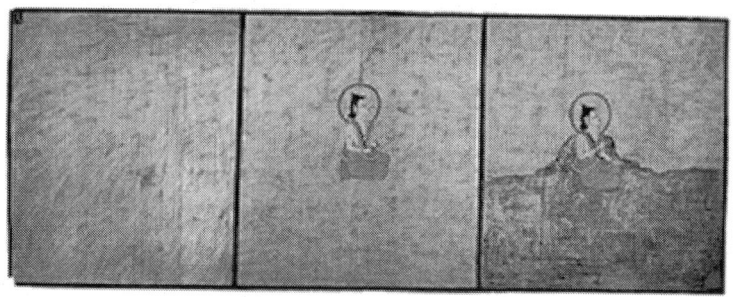

Symbols

The ancient *rishis* of India devoted a great deal of time to researching matters related to the invisible. The rich symbolism they left behind was intended to illustrate every spiritual realization, bringing the subtle into the physical. The symbol was the means of holding a mental image or feeling; it was believed to act as a support and to stimulate the mind to cause the reemergence of a given experience. Today, the multiple visual references found in Hinduism can be confusing because sacred images and signs have passed through successive interpretations and often lost their original meaning.

One of the symbols portrayed most often is the soul. In most places of worship we still find oval-shaped stones and images. These are called *lingam* and originally served to symbolize a form as invisible as the atom: the soul as perceived in meditative insights—a self-luminous point. Another representation is the "third eye"—the mark or dot on the forehead. Even though people still wear the *bindi*, few are aware of its symbolic relation to the imperishable self.

Shiva Paramatma—the Supreme Soul—has often been portrayed in the form of light. The word *Shiva* means both "point" and "benefactor," beautifully describing the form and main attribute of the one God. It is believed that the word *Shiva* was later echoed in the Hebrew YHVH—the *Jehovah* of Abraham.

The oval-shaped *Shivalingam* is found in many temples and is frequently surrounded by smaller *saligrams,* representing a parental relationship. The Supreme Soul is also reflected in the Sanskrit word *Deus Peter,* which was taken to Greece as *Zeus Pater* and later translated by the Romans as *Jupiter.*

Swastika

The *swastika* was used as a sacred sign by many cultures. The oldest *swastikas* have been found in ancient sites like Mohenjo-daro, Harappa, and the Sarasvati Valley, as well as in Persia and Mesopotamia. In Turkey, it was customary to place it inside graves. In ancient Italy and Greece, it was used to ensure the welfare of the dead. In India as well as in Greece, there were *swastika* coins, and among the Celts and Egyptians it was used as a religious sign from as early as the first dynasties. The symbol was also found in the

Roman Empire, including in England and Ireland as well as in China. It was widely spread throughout the Far East through Buddhism and was also commonly used by the native inhabitants of the Americas. Early Christians also used the *swastika* on their graves, a custom that was later replaced by the symbol of the cross.

The *swastika* is still used to convey many meanings, such as good fortune and auspicious omens, and is believed to be related to God or the Creator. In India's traditional literature, the *swastika* represents four directions or paths—*chatushpatha*. Its four arms, pointing clockwise, indicate a pattern of circular motion. Its division into four ages, or *yugas,* refers to actual periods of history that have a direct connection with different stages of consciousness.

Many of the symbols India created and once sustained have now been scattered or distanced from their original meaning. However, they can be perceived and understood when placed within the cyclic perspective, because this view brings the contents of many primordial signs and images to light.

Home

It was a dimension of light, a space where we resided as if floating in a state of inner fulfillment. Without a body, the soul experienced deep inner silence. There was no impulse of action, no need for thoughts. There was peace.

Just as the physical world exists in an element called *akash*, or ether, the highest subtle realm similarly exists in a principle or substance called *Akand Jyoti Maha Tattwa*— divine infinite light. This is our original home. It has been remembered as *Nirvana*, the realm beyond sound, and also as *Brahmand*, the land of subtle light.

This dimension extends far beyond the limits of outer space. While resting in the highest region, the soul has no mental or sensory experiences, nor is it lost or dissolved in an ocean of diffuse light. It is in a place of absolute silence.

Before we manifest our inner qualities, they are latent, as if awaiting a cue—or the right moment we can begin playing our part on this world stage.

"...Suddenly, quite unnoticed, I stood on this other earth in bright sunlight of a day as beautiful as paradise...Oh, everything was exactly as on our earth, but it seemed that everything around radiated with some holiday, and with great, holy and finally achieved triumph. The calm emerald sea gently splashed against the shore embracing it with manifest, apparent, almost conscious love. Tall beautiful trees stood there in full luxury of their bloom, and their countless leaflets - I am sure of it - welcomed me with great, gentle, kind murmur, uttering, as it were, words of love. The grass sparkled with bright fragrant flowers. Little birds, in flocks, flew through the air, and, unafraid of me, alighted on my shoulders and hands, joyfully beating at me with dear little trepidating wings.

And, finally, I saw and got to know the people of that happy land. They came to me themselves, they surrounded and embraced me. Children of the sun; of their sun. Oh, how beautiful they were! Never did I see on our earth such beauty in man. Perhaps only in our children of most tender age is it possible to find a remote reflection of that beauty. The eyes of those happy people were full of bright glitter. Their faces radiated with intelligence and some kind of consciousness which had reached the level of tranquility; yet those faces were cheerful. Innocent gladness sounded in the words and voices of those men.

Oh, at once, at the first glance of those faces, I grasped everything, everything! This was an earth not defiled by sin; upon it lived men who had not sinned; they lived in a paradise similar to that in which, according to the tradition of all mankind, lived our fallen forefathers...

...Oh, I understood at once, that in many respects I should not comprehend them at all...It seemed incredible, for instance, that they, who knew so much, did not possess our science. But soon I came to understand that their knowledge was amplified by and derived from revelations which differed from those on our earth, and that their aspirations were altogether different. They had no desires and they were placid; they did not aspire to the knowledge of life, as we seek to explain what life is; science itself endeavors to conceive it in order to teach others how to live; they, however, knew how to live, and this I understood...

...They were vivacious and joyous like children. They roamed through their beautiful groves and forests; they sang lovely songs; they subsisted on light food, on fruits from their trees, on honey from the woods, on the milk of animals which loved them. They labored but little and slighted for their food and clothing. They were endowed with love, and children were born to them, but never did I observe in them those impulses of cruel voluptuousness which affect virtually everybody on our earth - everybody, and which are the sole source of almost all sin in our human race. They rejoiced over their newborn as new participants in their felicity. They never quarreled and there was no jealousy amongst them; they did not even understand what these things meant.

There were virtually no diseases among them, although there was death. However, their old men passed away gently, as though falling asleep, surrounded by men bidding them farewell, blessing them, smiling to them; and they departed accompanied by serene smiles. On these occasions I perceived no sorrow, no tears; there was merely love grown to the level of ecstasy...

..They were so unaccountably convinced of an eternal life that it did not constitute a question to them. They had no temples, but in them there was some kind of a daily, live, unceasing communion with the whole of the universe. They glorified nature, the earth and seas and forests. They were fond of composing songs about one another; they praised each other like children. Those were the simplest songs, but they evoked them from the heart and penetrated it. And not only in songs, but it seemed they were spending all their lives in admiring each other. It was a sort of mutual, complete and universal captivation.

— *The Dream of a Ridiculous Man* - Fyodor Dostoevsky

Sat Yuga

The Golden Age — the first quarter of the cycle — is believed to be the peak of human civilization. This is when the world experienced a culture without parallel in history.

The Age of Truth is symbolized by wisdom and virtue in might; a time when natural ethics ruled and the Dharma was common to all.

Self-rule and the full expression of one's potential were the birthright of every soul. Their inner light and love became the sustaining core of a great kingdom. These were "sixteen celestial degrees" humans, as complete as the full moon. This age is remembered as Paradise.

The reminiscence of this period remains incognito yet alive in every temple of India.

"First flowered the age of gold, which, while it knew nor judge nor law, was freely just and true. No penalties were fixed; no threats appeared graven on bronze to make stern edicts feared; no judges' words dismayed the suppliant throng; without protectors all were safe from wrong. No swords were forged, no soldier plied his trade; men lived at peace, carefree and unafraid; unscarred by plows, and by no contract tied, earth, of her bounty, every need supplied. Spring was eternal, earth a garden, blessed with blooms unsown, which temperate winds caressed; in fields untilled the bursting ears were seen, and yellowing harvest where no plows had been; and streams of milk and nectar flowing free; and gold in green, the honey in the tree."

– Metamorphoses, Book One - Ovid

More than a myth or ideal belonging to the imagination of ancient peoples, the perfect age was believed to have really existed. The celebrated Eden of ancient cultures — preserved in the memorials of great civilizations as well as in popular folklore — has come down to us as fragmented memories from a distant era. The constant mention of elevated ancestors and the nostalgic narrative of the beginning of time, when a few of the divinely gifted were made instruments of creation, is part of a universal repository of thoughts on the origin of humanity.

Every creative impulse in history, every new philosophy and ideology, every religious or cultural manifestation has contained a deep desire, often unconscious, for the heavenly ideal: a return to high consciousness, to a harmonious order and liberation from suffering. Inside the core of all these there remained a latent desire for *jeevan-mukti*—a life of constant happiness.

The narratives and allegories that describe life in the first age are innumerable. According to Chuang Tzu, a Chinese Taoist philosopher:

> *They were upright and correct, without knowing that to be so was righteousness; they loved one another, without knowing that to do so was benevolence; they were honest and loyal-hearted without knowing that it was loyalty; they fulfilled their engagement, without knowing that to do so was good faith; in their simple movements they employed the services of one another, without thinking that they were conferring or receiving any gift. Therefore their actions left no trace, and there was no record of their affairs.*
>
> **— Myths of China and Japan - Donald A. Mackenzie**

The Bible also describes episodes from man's sovereignty over the world:

> *"And the Lord God planted a garden in Eden, in the direction of the East, and placed them there." "...And God said, let them rule over the fishes of the sea and over the birds of the sky, and over the cattle and over the earth and over all the reptiles that move on earth."*
>
> *— Genesis II: 8; I:26,27*

Indian history is full of quotations and images that echo the collective memory of a time when people were as noble in their conduct as they were materially developed. Dispersed records exist of this historical period in all ancient scriptures, including the *Vedas*, which are considered to be the oldest documents in the Indo-European tradition.

The ancient cyclic perspective opens up a historical gap that stands entirely opposed to the more recent theory of evolution. All ancient sources, whether Indian, Egyptian, Greek, or Persian, have made use of this reference, which later became the foundation for many religions and cults.

According to this vision, the first age of the world represents the peak of human experience. As time passes by, the degrees of perfection gradually reduce as part of a natural process that culminates in a complete inversion of the experiences and values of the beginning age.

> *"The Perfect Age was so called because there was only one Dharma and all men were saints; this is why there was no need for religious rituals. There were neither gods nor demons. Their main virtue was the absence of all mundane desires. Kriya Yuga -- the Perfect Age -- had no sickness, there was no depreciation as time went by; there was neither hate nor vanity or any kind of bad thoughts, sadness or fear..."*
>
> *— Mahabharat, Santiparvan Moksadharma - 231-23*

"There, people were divine and their thoughts were fulfilled" (Rig Veda 55.6); "They possessed great spiritual power and were righteous" (Vrihat Sanhpita 1.1 Utpal Tika); "They were born through the power of yoga and left their bodies also through the power of yoga" (Vayu Purana 65.112 and 71.61-63); "and because their bodies were created through the power of yoga, they were healthy and without sicknesses."(Shvetashvatara Upanishad 2.12); "Only those who were spiritually great deserved to be born and were born in Sat Yuga, which was the very creation of God." (Satyarth Prakash)

Focusing most of the narrative in India, we can only reach back a certain distance, finding a people whose ancestors left no records of their past. Considered the world's oldest religion, even Hinduism itself can neither trace its origins nor name its founders.

In their first records, the people of Bharat already claimed descent from a superior civilization, which they called *Adi Sanatam Devi Devata Dharma* — the Ancient and Original Deity Dharma.

Dharma is a word that defies easy translation. In essence, it means to live according to the laws and principles that govern nature.

India's cultural and spiritual heritage still carries fragments of this "prehistoric" past. When memories started fading, sages laid down the foundation of a social structure in order to prevent further decline. The aim seems to have

The Cycle of Time

been to restore the previous condition of perfection, which, despite their efforts, was never to return. Their ideal has survived to today through their beautiful memorials of ancient deities.

Bharat

The Golden Age witnessed the ascension of a dynasty whose emperors personified the most elevated human attributes.

Deities were human beings who embodied the highest qualities. Their greatest treasure was their minds, through which they experienced a constant exchange of happiness. Their internal stability and peace generated an environment of receptivity and care. Because of the pure atmosphere, thoughts could travel long distances, delivering messages or images to others. One needed only a clear intellect to receive them.

They were neither saints nor scholars, but simple and naturally noble people. Wisdom and integrity were inherent in them, and no gurus or spiritual preceptors were ever needed. They understood the relationship between mind, body, and the material universe. Theirs were lives with no hard work, neither for the body nor for the intellect, in which being awake and being asleep were equally comfortable.

The knowledge science produces, in its most advanced form, was available through the minds of a select few. Scientists brought knowledge of the material world within their souls, in the same way that musicians and artisans already possessed the skills of their arts and the king had already perfected the *sanskaras* of running a kingdom. The relationship between mind and body was no less refined, leaving behind stories of lifetimes without disease.

They lived in the peace of a non-divided kingdom, with no thoughts of invading each other's inner realms.

Their faces reflected their innocence and self-respect. They communicated using gracious movements: a glance could express a feeling; a gesture could express the clarity of an idea. There were no words to indicate opposites or duality of will; words were self-explanatory, filled with significance and good feelings.

In the Golden Age, everyone possessed natural beauty. Even in old age, faces remained cheerful; bodies had flexibility and lightness, and eyes were filled with love. Those eyes were windows into their inner world, reflecting what life is meant to be. This is why crowds are still drawn to see their memorials in the temples, hoping for a mere glimpse of their images.

Clothing was rich and colorful and signified both the position and the occupation people had in the kingdom. Lifespans were long, and they could always tell when the moment for departing was near. Leaving a body was planned in the same way one plans a journey. Because they had no burdens or attachment to what was left behind, their departure was safe and painless, as when one falls into a deep sleep.

Deities were light in the substance of their bodies. Their inner purity emerged as a light that divinized them. Even today they are referred to as *devas*—the "shining ones."

They were noble and self-sovereign, which accounts for their rule being the most legitimate and benevolent of all time. They had no police to enforce the law, no military or defense projects. Counselors to the king were also unnecessary. The king and queen were partners in the administration of the state. *Hukam hazur ka raj rani ka*: "The king's order and the queen's system were the way of ruling" when *Divya Mariada*—a "divine order"—ruled the world.

It was customary for kings to call the royal assembly together and celebrate the prince's coronation when the king reached old age. In the ceremony, the prince was given a *tilak* — a dot on the forehead — as a sign of the powers of self-governing, and the crown was passed on as a symbol of the sovereignty of the state.

Their character could be seen in their relationship with all living things. Food was never a product of killing, and their love turned them into guardians of nature. The spirituality and wisdom these souls had developed were intuitively manifested.

The deities were aware of the impermanence of their bodies but had no knowledge of past and future. They recognized each other's virtues and did not long for anything, for every possible experience was available to them.

Masculine and feminine attributes were perfectly matched in each couple, whose union was the basis of harmony in the community. The image of *Vishnu* was left as a symbol of perfection and balance between the masculine and the feminine in the human soul, as well as the love that made two into one.

Couples were partners in the conception of children, whom they created through the mind. The basis of creation was thought. This art of silent communication was called *yoga*. Thus, a child conceived by the power of *yoga* was especially desired and always welcomed. Due to this power they were called *ajar* (unborn) and *amar* (immortal).

The lightness and brightness of the world reflected their state of inner perfection. Nature was generous and abundant, with a variety of flowers and fruits of extraordinary quality. It didn't take long for things to grow, and the fertile ground provided for them without demanding much labor. Flowers, fruits, and grains were used as food, and "rivers of milk and honey" flowed. There were different kinds of fruits; some were used for juices, others as spices. The elements of nature were in their purest, *satoguni* state.

Their water came from mineralized springs, becoming fragrant and medicinal as it passed through the mountains' herbs. There were mines for gold and precious gems in many places, making it possible to use these resources even in the decoration of palaces and houses.

There were no temples at this time, no sacred books; divinity was naturally manifested, and *Dharma* was the way of life.

Births, weddings, and coronations were occasions for celebration, and everyone had artistic skills. Study encompassed music, painting, and games; even history was taught through poems and songs. Some games were played in the form of dances, and theaters were spread throughout the kingdom.

The *Chakravartins*—"rulers of the globe"—lived life with no boundaries. They traveled long distances in fast and safe aircraft. Technology was extremely sophisticated, and energy was obtained from natural sources, including atomic energy.

The whole kingdom operated as a family, in which giving and taking was but a mutual exchange. Most things were produced in abundance, and business existed in the form of sharing or trade. Communities were small and people were very close to one another. Nothing was ever lacking; everyone owned more than they needed.

Property was felt to be held in common, and all dealings were based on a sense of community and belonging. For this reason, records and accounts were hardly needed. It was a perfect life—the Golden Age.

The Cycle of Time

Treta Yuga

Time flows in a descending movement as entropy gradually sets in. The soul continues its journey, being born and reborn in the cycle of life. The world continuously moves away from the highest stage experienced during the first age.

The Silver Age was still a time of great fruition. Thoughts were expressions of the spirit in lifetimes of great beauty. For this reason, "three quarters" — *treta* — of the moonlight were still seen.

It is the rule of the Moon Dynasty whose memorials are depicted in most Indian arts.

"But one day the king and the queen found themselves in another land. Another dress and different faces with which they expressed their love, and though their life was good and all the courtiers smiled, a moment came when something changed. A single thought had lost itself between the mind of the king and the mind of the queen. Because of that a flicker of doubt crossed the face of the subject in front of them and she went away with a question in her mind. And it was called a Silver Age.

And within the mother - the subject who had knelt before them - the question played its own game and hardly without knowing it she turned her head and looked with too much love as her child prepared to leave. A tiny seed of damage had been sewn.

And the seed became a leaf and as the gardener dug his land he spotted it as it floated down the river. A single leaf had fallen from the tree though the summer hadn't yet gone, and within the sight he felt a signal that the nature which he understood and loved was changing.

And as he walked, the music played, the musician sang his songs. But just once he pushed his voice too far and the note he sang slipped slightly out of key. It was the beginning of an interference between the creator and his creation, the singer and his songs.

But the change was so very slight that they did not even know. As the queen ruled, the mother loved, the farmer farmed and the musician played, they did not see the moon waning in the sky. Not until the light began to dim did they notice that they could not see."

– *Olympia* - **Anthea Church**

The Expansion of the Kingdom

The first dynasty ruled for generations when the government was passed on to another family. The new kings and queens inherited a kingdom still living the same *Dharma*.

The population had grown bigger, and though everything ran smoothly with little effort, there was still an order holding things together. This was most apparent in people's inherent qualities. With the expansion of the population, the varying degrees of perfection stood out, becoming visible in everyone's talents. The ages of Paradise displayed the color and beauty of diversity based on natural gifts and inclinations. The most elevated *sanskaras* as well as the soul's full potential had been expressed during the first age. The Silver Age *reflected* that initial period.

In this simple yet advanced culture, relationships continued to be based on trust. Because of their dignity and honesty, there were no expectations, distrust, or need for recognition. Communities were organized and sustained by self-realized beings, and contentment and peace was experienced according to each one's nature.

Geographic and climatic conditions were stable during the first half of the world cycle. There was one main continent, a mass of land surrounded by seas and islands. The seasons were mild, and nature provided more than enough for consumption. Cities were small and beautifully gardened. Communication in and between cities was easy and fast by air, sea, or land.

This period is remembered as *Vaikunth*, "the celestial realm" on earth. Embodying virtues and qualities of the highest level, royalty was the sustaining core of values and customs. Their inner strength helped preserve a system that would later turn into a variety of traditions.

Power wasn't conferred simply through external titles; it originated from the depths of the soul. Hereditary succession only confirmed the potential and *karmic* destiny of souls who naturally possessed the *sanskaras* of self-mastery, wisdom, and love.

* * *

No records or physical ruins of this period have survived. The few texts that have come down to us belong to a later generation, and they are often coded or already intertwined with myth. Details about the lives and fate of the peoples who lived before the floods remain mysterious. We do find tales about the wonders of Bharat, Atlantis, and the land of Kemet, which often refer to their inhabitants' psychic capacities, highly developed cities, and advanced technologies.

In the Silver Age, new populations had already started to appear in different lands, bringing with them the memory and customs of their common ancestors. Even though the age of perfection was over, the following generations put their efforts into keeping and adapting the old systems.

The ancient Egyptians, for example, knew that their culture and traditions originated from a divine race that existed before the age of the pharaohs. They called their eight ancestor deities "the august shebtiu"—the senior ones, "the children of Tjenen" (of the risen land), the offspring of the Creator, Atum, and the glorious spirits of the early primeval age.

As time went on, there continued to be interaction, assimilation, and transformation in all living things. Everything is constantly subjected to change. The process of birth and rebirth and the growing exchange among an increasing number of people made the soul move away from its original state of completeness.

What was at first an imperceptible and unconscious process eventually created space for the first bits of instability to emerge. A spiritual decline had gradually set in; a very subtle movement began to take shape within the human psyche.

There came a point when the inner light of the soul could no longer support the self or sustain a peaceful world.

The Fall

> *"And then every sin broke loose upon this age, and honor and truth fled hence, and in their place there sprang up every form of wrong and deceit, and treachery and brute force and the cursed lust of gain. Their canvas they set to the winds, of which the sailor as yet knew little...That soil which had been once shared by all, even as the sun's rays and the breezes, the niggard land-surveyor now marked out with long-drawn balks.*
>
> *No longer did men demand from the rich soil only its crops and the food that is their due, but to the earth's very vitals they pushed, and quarried out the treasures which she had hidden and stored away hard by the nether gloom. By this time baleful still; then came war that arms herself with both, and with blood stained hands clashes her ringing panoply..."*
>
> *— Metamorphoses, Book One - Ovid*

Having lost his spiritual identity and strength, man began to experience suffering. A change in consciousness affected his perception and expression. Emotional pain and unfulfilled desire became part of the play. The inner power that had sustained them for so long gave way to fear, aversion, and anger. Mental turmoil began to manifest itself.

Identification with the temporary and perishable resulted in feelings of possession and ego. The capacity for seeing beyond, that super-sensorial perception, disappeared.

> "The Lord then said to Adam: When you were subjected to me, you possessed a bright inner nature, and for this reason you could see things from a distance. But after your transgression, this bright nature was taken from you; and you could not see distant things but only that which was close, within the reach of your hand, according to the capacity of flesh, which is gross..."
>
> – *The Forgotten Books of Eden*

Along with inner purity, man also lost his divine powers. Dissociated from his original nature, he now faced limitations in reasoning and perspective. The desire to recover was there, but the Fall was not solely an internal process, for it was followed by the disintegration of the whole system. Life could no longer be predicted; the certainty and stability they had enjoyed for generations was no more. The ancients were witness to a complete reversal of nature, which until then had reflected only man's non-violence.

> "The divine portion that existed in them was now tenuous and debilitated by having mingled to a great quantity of mortality..."

> *"There were then earthquakes and floods of extraordinary violence, and in a single dreadful day and night all men were swallowed up by the sea and vanished..."*
>
> *– Timaeus - Plato*

This period left traumatic impressions on the human soul. Everything changed: longevity was reduced and untimely death became a reality. Attachment to the physical and impermanent, things like appearance and status, proved deceptive. A physical or material sense of self sprouted negativities that opened the season of human suffering.

> *"I give you all plants that bear seed everywhere on earth, and every tree bearing fruit which yields seed: they shall be yours for food. All green plants I give for food to the wild animals, to all the birds of heaven, and to all reptiles on earth, every living creature."*
>
> *– Genesis 1:29*

But now, *"every creature that lives and moves shall be food for you now, I give you them all, as once I gave you all green plants."* And therefore, *"fear and dread of you shall fall upon all wild animals on earth, on all birds of heaven, on everything that moves upon the ground and all fish of the sea..."*

– Genesis 9:2.3

Actions motivated by negativity and selfish desires were now acceptable, and the concepts of sin and guilt arose as experiences of *karmic* return. Customs and systems were rapidly transforming together with man's condition:

> *Now we cannot see as before: our eyes have become of flesh, they cannot see in the way they could... What is today our body compared to what it was previously, when we used to live in the garden?"*
>
> **– The Forgotten Books of Eden**

The changes in the minds of men were echoed in the very structure of nature. For the first time, huge calamities showed the full force of the elements. Earthquakes and tsunamis swept the continents, leaving no trace of Golden Dwarka or the lost land of Atlantis.

Global cataclysms tore continents apart, creating new land, mountains, and seas. A deviation in the planet's tilt resulted in a change in the axis and the gravitational field of the earth. Geophysical features, the flora and the fauna, were greatly altered. Genetic mutations occurred and new species appeared.

"Among other things, there was the drying up of great oceans, the falling away of mountain peaks, the deviation of the fixed pole-star, the cutting of the wind-cords (of the stars), the submergence of the earth, the retreat of the celestials from their station."

— Maitri Upanishad 4

"These were the families of the sons of Noah according to their genealogies, nation by nation; and from them came the separate nations on earth after the flood...And the entire world spoke a single language and used the same words. As men journeyed from the East, they came upon a plain in the land of Shinar and settled there."

— Genesis 10:32; 11:1,2

The ancient land was destroyed; some parts sank into the ocean while others were torn apart by continental streams. The survivors were geographically scattered, as few managed to migrate to safe lands. Accounts of massive floods are part of the creation stories of all ancient cultures. Those who became aware of the impending doom seem to have been the most prepared.

The Beginning of Memory

Moved by distress and wonder, people sought to understand the new patterns, the reality behind the changes in the cosmic order. A great power had certainly been manifested. Varuna, Indra, Brahma... the mystery had to be comprehended. The quest was about to begin.

> "...It was then that men started to call out the name of God"
>
> – *Genesis IV.2*

Inner conflict along with devastating calamities caused an previously unknown instinct to arise. Man began to see the forces of nature as a power connected to and yet greater than him.

This is recorded history. When people started to talk about the "gods," they no longer existed. And when temples, pyramids, and sacrificial fires were later built and dedicated to the ancient deities, they were based on memories of a lost past.

The limits between recorded history and the obscure periods of prehistory have reached us through these narratives, which contain but fragments of the collective remembrance of the first age. Often in archetypal form, these stories tell us about a period of perfection and its disappearance:

> "He, who knew the seas and the countries of the world, he was wise, he saw the mysteries, and knew the secret things, he brought us a tale of the days before the flood.
>
> He went a long journey, was weary, worn out with labor, and returning engraved on a stone the whole story..."
>
> – *The Epic of Gilgamesh*

The Old Testament describes this time as a transition between the divine and the human, when "gods" saw that "the daughters of men" had beauty and took them as wives, and "children began dying before their parents" as "death entered the world."

> "In those days, when the sons of God had relationship with the daughters of men and got children of them; they became the heroes of old, men of renown."
>
> – *Genesis V.4*

These "giants" of knowledge, who could live up to 120 years, were the first sages and kings who were to shape the social structure that followed.

However, this period also marks the end of perennial peace and happiness. The next generation still heard about the changes and migrations, the floods and earthquakes witnessed by their people.

> "I soon realized that the ancient sages lived in a frightened state of mind, justified by the events they or their close ancestors had witnessed. The ancients' message was an anguished effort to communicate their awe engendered at seeing nature with its elements unchained."
>
> — **Immanuel Velikovsky - In the Beginning**

The last generations of the Silver Age had left a legacy of warnings, besides reminders of a rich and profound knowledge. They sufficed to give an initial impulse to sciences and philosophies that later blossomed into extraordinary cultures dispersed through all the continents. This knowledge was used for building monuments, astronomic observatories, and calendars that still amaze the world.

It didn't take long for religious traditions to appear, as man was still trying to preserve the legacy and *Dharma* of his ancestors.

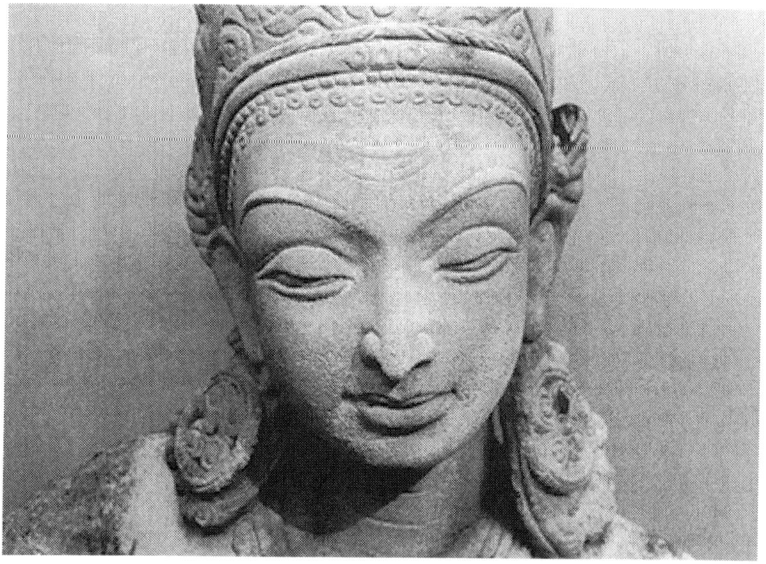

Dwapur Yuga

The Copper Age begins as a moment of transition—it is when history changed its course as man inverted his values. Ancient texts speak of the Fall of humanity, of limitations and bondage that prevent the soul from experiencing truth and freedom. Perfection, previously experienced in mind and body, becomes a mere ideal projected onto a mystical horizon.

This period marks the beginning of the search for a Supreme Being as a possible source for lost knowledge and power. *Dwapur Yuga* is represented by the long and varied journey of spiritual paths, which is still a feature of India and its people.

Realization and beauty were still related then to the metaphysical and the spiritual. Despite the existence of duality, there were still eight "celestial degrees" of light in the human soul.

"Maybe that which most impresses us as we read the hymns of the Vedas, is that instead of being commandments prescribed by priests or prophets, they bring us a poetical testament of the collective reaction of a people before the wonder and awe of existence. A people of vigorous and genuine imagination, awaken by a feeling of the inexhaustible mystery implicit in life. It was a simple faith of theirs that has attributed divinity to each element and force of nature, a courageous and joyful faith, in which the fear of the gods was balanced by confidence, in which the feeling of mystery only brought enchantment to life, without the burden of perplexity...

The first authors were almost childish in their reactions, fascinated by what they observed, and naively searching to adjust that to their own hopes and fears. But as children grow up and gain a broader perception of themselves, the later authors searched more and more to a centre of reference in their own consciousness, a subjective correlative to the greatness that has kept them for so long captivated, an answer in their own being to the cosmic challenge of the visible universe..."

– *The Hindu Scriptures - Introduction by Rabindranath Tagore*

Beginning Once Again

According to the cyclic perspective, the movements of history are triggered by changes in the human soul, a process that influences and transforms customs and systems.

As long as our perception is capable of acknowledging subtle levels of thinking, and as long as we live in line with our highest self, the potential energy of mind and intellect is unlimited.

As we move away from our souls, we are limited to what reaches us through the senses and the external world. The power of knowing and controlling the mind is weakened. Soul consciousness is eventually replaced by the limitations of the physical brain and body.

The imbalance of human consciousness over a period of time was seen as directly affecting the very structure of the planet. Huge cataclysms followed, causing new continents to emerge after earthquakes and tsunamis.

The internal purity and integrity of the human soul has sustained the field of energy—the core of material life—for half the cycle. Prolonged loss of self-control ended up producing unpredictable events. These changes also affected the body, which began to experience illness and anomalies. Special techniques were developed in order to alleviate physical pain and deficiencies. Research into the interaction between mind and body began.

In many parts of the world, efforts were made to reduce or prevent further calamities. There was still a level of information, a knowledge that would soon become inaccessible because it combined not only mathematics and geometry, gravity and electromagnetic fields, but also the interactive process between mind and matter. One such example is the construction of pyramids, where huge stone blocks were carved and transported using highly sophisticated techniques derived from principles ignored by subsequent generations.

Work no longer expressed the highest abilities of the self but became a means of survival. The human intellect would soon compensate for the weakening of its natural capacities by developing new inventions.

It was in this period that the first records of Indian history appeared, giving rise to the Vedas, Upanishads, and other Sanskrit texts, many of them still untranslated.

New sciences and schools of thought also started to develop. In the field of mathematics, the decimal system of notation, the concept of zero, the value of the infinite, the extraction of square and cube roots, the rule of three, and the precise value of *pi* are some of India's legacies.

Through astronomy and advancements in the field of trigonometry, spherical geometry and calculus were developed. Many civilizations of that time were able to draw the zodiac; to study the rotation of and gravitational influences on planets; and to compute eclipse cycles, precession, and retrogression. In the medical field, the Indian Ayurvedic treatises comprised an extensive study of herbs, minerals, and organic functions.

Throughout this period, the intelligent minds of India searched for the answers to the mysteries of life. An entire culture laid its foundation on the many interpretations of an ultimate reality. Sciences and philosophies tried to understand the forces behind the movements of nature. Self-analysis developed along with speculation on observed effects. Was there a unique essence that had been transmuted? Were the forces of individual life actually derived from it?

> "But after all, who knows, and who can say from where it all came, and how creation happened? The gods themselves are later than creation, so who knows truly when it has arisen?"
>
> – Rig Veda X, 129

> "Some sages say that inherent nature, others that time, is this world's cause. Both are mistaken. It is the grandeur of God within this world by which this wheel of Brahman is made to turn... Let us know the most elevated Lord of the lords, the Master of Masters; the highest on high, as God -- the Lord of the World, the Adorable. There is neither cause nor effect for Him, nobody is like Him; His power is revealed in many forms, it is inherent and it acts as strength and knowledge..."
>
> – Svetasvatara Upanishad VI, 1

In an attempt to understand and control his physical surroundings, man developed his capacity of observation and abstract reasoning. Astronomy and astrology were integrated into metaphysical thought. Life was ruled by the rhythm of nature, and those who observed it came to realize the dimension of their being within a vast and unlimited plan. They revered the sacred nature of existence and in this way sustained their devotion to the spiritual.

Despite their loss of inner strength, a few people were still able to produce supernatural phenomena. Esoteric and magical orders arose, some for selfish purposes. Beliefs and cults formed around whatever remained of ancient knowledge:

> *"That self is hidden in all beings and don't irradiate, but it is seen by the subtle seer through his sharp and subtle intellect. A sage should reserve himself in his mind and speech; should keep the knowledge inside himself who is grandiose; and should keep the self silent. The one who has perceived that which has no sound, no touch, no form, that which does not decay, which is tasteless, eternal, without smell, without beginning, without end, is free of the claws of death. And the one who repeats this great mystery in the assembly of the Brahmins, or with total devotion at the time of the sacrifice of Sraddha, obtains infinite rewards..."*
>
> *– Katha Upanishad - Third Valli*

"Tat Savitur Varenyam"
We meditate before that adorable light...

– *Brihadaranyaka Upanishad*

Bhakti – Paths of Devotion

Somnath was one of the most beloved temples in all of India, and according to old records, one of the wealthiest. Its story is similar to those of other shrines built over the period; these were places sought for their aura of peace, and they became centers of learning and tradition for many communities.

Emblematic of the power of faith, the story of Somnath may be used to represent the apex and fall in the history of devotion. When the temple complex was first attacked, it was served by over a thousand *Brahmin* priests, besides hundreds of musicians, astronomers, dancers, and servers, and was sustained by donations from more than ten thousand towns.

Ancient accounts speak of three thousand camels being needed to transport its treasures. The incursion left more than fifty thousand victims. But it was more than lives and wealth that was lost. The event was a turning point in the fate of a land then edging into the uncertainty of medieval times.

The origin of Somnath is obscure and permeated by myth. It was said to be built by a legendary king named Vikramaditya in a time when most kingdoms were beginning their quest to understand and preserve an ancient heritage. This was the trend everywhere, giving rise to a variety of spiritual paths in all continents. India was where the silent practices of meditation and spiritual *yoga* were born, and it became famous for the depth of its inquiries into the nature of consciousness and its search for the Divine.

The destruction of a number of Hindu temples many generations later seemed to indicate the end of this era. Peace of mind was becoming an ideal rather than a common experience.

Somnath, "the Lord of Nectar," was dedicated to Incorporeal Shiva. *Soma* was connected with the moon because their practice began early, when the moon was still shining. Being awake before sunrise is a tradition still preserved in temples and ashrams. Besides love and devotion, discipline was the foundation for the many insights and inner capacities ancient sages possessed. Even the drinking of soma, a ritual plant elixir, was done within this context, with the aim of attaining spiritual realization and self-control.

Somnath used to be the wonder of India. In its central dome a suspended oval-shaped jewel symbolized "the One without an Image." *Koh-i-noor*, the "Mountain of Light," a famous 108-carat diamond, is said to have been part of this original *lingam*.

Temples built during this period were inlayed with gold and precious gems donated by the greatest kings and patrons in the course of many centuries. Royal families devoted much of their possessions toward the foundation of shrines and spiritual institutions. There was still genuine interest in the metaphysical aspects of life. India was famous in antiquity for its development of theories about the universe and the nature of consciousness, and until recently her spiritual heritage was the most profound philosophical investigation in human thought.

Entire generations were inspired to carry on systems and practices with the intention of maintaining the principles that governed the world. Knowing one's self and realizing the true nature of the Supreme were considered the highest goals. Turning to *Dharma* meant understanding and bringing out the qualities and talents that made life worth living.

The rulers of India were duty-bound to protect the systems created by the *Brahmin* sages. The priests, in turn, performed their role on the basis of a legacy they sought to understand and preserve. Their inherited knowledge was the sustaining core of temporal power, and it managed to hold an already fragmented system in relative unity.

This was possible because India was once the home of an extraordinary civilization based on universal harmony and creative abundance. It was this nostalgic past, governed by the legendary *Chakravartins*—the universal rulers of the first age—that kept the memory of deities alive.

"When you see his face, praise him with joy,
Adore him with joined palms, bow before him,
so that his feet touch your head."

– *Pattuppattu, Tirumuruganarrupadai*
Tamil Devotional Poem

Images of ancient rulers became symbols of spiritual achievements. The attributes of perfection returned, carved in stone. Beautiful statues, richly decorated, became objects of devotion. A collective invocation of Paradise—the lost Kingdom of *Sat Yuga*—was born.

Varying manifestations of search and devotion would soon branch into different paths. All emerging civilizations were then establishing their own particular worldview and religious code. No other place, however, synthesizes this period so well as India, for here the memorials of a perfect world were born and have been kept alive up to today.

Kala - The Spirit in the Art

> "The celebrated beginning to the ancient text of the Vishnudharmottaram describes the predicament of the king who wished to learn the art of painting -- chitra kala. He was informed that to paint, to render figures in plastic volume, he must first learn to sculpt. To attempt sculpture, to understand gesture and movement, he must apply himself first to the principles of dance. And to dance he must have recourse to the appreciation of rhythm, of tala -- of instrumental and then vocal music. And music, of course, seeks its inspiration from poetry. Thus the king learnt that to be skilled in one of the arts, he must be informed about all of them."
>
> — *Rasa* - *Mandakini Trivedi*

Indian culture was impregnated with spiritual motifs, with inspiration drawn from devotional feelings. The arts still expressed joy and recognized the beauty of life, and creative thought was naturally spiritual and filled with enthusiasm.

Art was mostly dedicated to revealing the divine nature of ancient deities, often depicting them in abstract form: the body as a representation of the spirit, the face expressing withdrawal from the physical. Symbols were used to portray ideas and subtle meanings.

Verbal and visual expression in the form of myths, folktales, and religion provided a means of expressing feelings and thoughts about the divine. Mental visions were invoked in meditation with the purpose of obtaining *Samadhi*, a state of super-consciousness. Images could also represent a mental attitude or activity. The movement of the eyes, the smile and posture of a dancer's hand were ways of transmitting a message.

This deep understanding of emotion and the language of gesture came to be used in sculpture, dance, and theater.

> *"Rasa is the aesthetic experience of an artistically engendered emotion. Rasa cannot be experienced at the level of the mundane or the empirical, it belongs to the world of art. Life provides the raw material and actual experiences are the springboard for the artist, whose creation is unique and unlike anything in real life. It is this otherworldly -- alokik -- character of the aesthetic experience that Bharata,*

author of the Natya Shastra, has in mind when he describes the various features that contribute to the experience of rasa.

Rasa, according to Bharata, is a combination of vibhavas (determinants), anubhavas (consequents) and vyabhichari bhavas (transitory moods). The crucial difference between actual emotion and the aesthetic one is that while the cause and effects of worldly emotions are personal, the aesthetic mood suggests the universal through stylized depiction. While in real life, latent emotions -- vasanas -- are aroused by actual events with the involvement of the ego bringing pain, in art they are aroused by imaginary situations. Thus the act of detached contemplation of a mood is what makes the artistic experience delightful and even morally elevating.

For a work of art to have this element of the universal it must be motivated by sthayi bhava or a dominant mood, the transitory or minor ones serving only to embellish it.

Indian aesthetics, which has Hindu philosophy animating it, believes that in the endless cycle of birth and death we have had every imaginable experience. These experiences that form the fiber of life are not destroyed at death but remain as latent impressions in our subconscious (sanskaras). And only an art form that reflects this, is instantly identifiable with, because the spectator 'knows' these emotions.

— Rasa - Mandakini Trivedi

The images of deities have been depicted using a variety of symbols that indicate methods of spiritual empowerment. Seekers and devotees were not meant to be spectators at that time. They saw themselves reflected in their heroes and aimed to follow in their footsteps. By emulating the highest archetypes, their reality was amplified and made relevant.

The deity holds in her many arms weapons that are attributes of her divine personality. A discus spins in one hand, symbolizing her understanding of time, while her mace represents mastery over thoughts and actions. The lotus flower is symbolic of purity and the conch shell of her intellectual capacity for sharing spiritual wisdom. The bow and arrow represent her power to deal with the negative, while the trident represents the three existing realities: matter (*prakriti*), soul (*atma*), and Supreme Soul (*Paramatma*).

The spiritual power and nobility of the soul becomes visible through her aura and crown. The *bindi* on her forehead symbolizes control over mind, intellect, and inner traits. Her jewels, placed over specific *chakras,* symbolize her control over the physical senses.

Goddesses are frequently portrayed riding a tiger or a lion—evidence of their fearlessness and a reminder of their victory over the illusions created by ignorance.

Female deities are often called *Shivshaktis* because they are believed to have received their powers directly from God. They are also remembered for their capacity for surrender and renunciation and their potential for learning.

Deities are considered images of support—*Adhar Murat*—and methods of achieving fortune—*Takzir Takdir*. Devotees are used to facing long queues and withstanding extremes of cold and heat just for a glimpse of their images.

The eyes of these *devtas* are said to be like jewels—*nure ratan*. They reflect a state of soul consciousness in which the inner eye has realized the eternal self.

Ancient Deities

From the beginning of Dwapur Yuga, changes in geography caused the human tree to stretch its branches in all directions. Migrations carried traces of an ancient culture that mixed and developed into new customs, languages, and systems.

Travelers and explorers started coming to India, where they found a culture already conscious of its antiquity. Pilgrims and philosophers from China, Egypt, Greece, Persia, and other lands came in search of wealth and metaphysical knowledge. Early accounts tell of the generosity and spirituality of the people, the prosperity of the kingdoms, and the abundance of resources. Fa-Hien, a Chinese monk who lived in India around 400 CE, wrote:

> *"There was such peace and gentleness in the administration of India that no serious crime was seen. It was possible to travel from one place to another without the need of travel permits. Everyone was respectable and vegetarian; meat was only eaten by the lower castes."*

As Persians traveled through Sindh, they came into contact with the region's inhabitants and started to refer to them and their religious practices by the name of the local river. In their pronunciation, they became "Hindus." This is still what the inhabitants of the region—the ancient "sons of Bharat"—are known as today.

The manifold paths that took shape in this region originated in what was left from memories of an earlier stage of mankind. At this point there were already nothing but faded memories of *Adi Sanatana Devi Devata Dharma*, the "Ancient and Eternal Deity Dharma."

In fact, what has come down to us as Hinduism has its roots in a collective invocation of a long lost Golden Age, systematically remembered in Indian culture. The loss of the original *Dharma* and the many attempts to restore it formed the basis for this variety of spiritual manifestations, which in the course of time became known as the Hindu Dharma.

Ancestor worship traveled throughout the continents. Each culture reproduced or created its own version of history according to regional tendencies. The civilizations that directly or indirectly descended from the ancient trunk of humanity had, however, a few features in common. Life in the community was centered on its particular cosmogony. The new kingdoms considered their kings to be direct descendants of the gods. The first dynasties of antiquity maintained temporal as well as religious power. The kings were also priests and were considered noble souls capable of performing a double role.

In India, the crystallization of the caste system separated these two functions. The *Brahmins* became priests and educators, while the *Kshatriyas*, who were also strategists and warriors, became rulers. The sacred character conferred on the Pharaoh in Egypt, the Son of Heaven in China, and the Mikado in Japan was not conferred on the ruling *Kshatriya* caste. The *Brahmins*—supported by specific disciplines and codes of conduct—were entitled to play the role of intermediary with the spiritual world.

> "Through contemplating sense-objects inwardly, visualizing and brooding over them, one brings into existence attachment to the objects; out of attachment comes desire; from desire, fury, violent passion; from violent passion, bewilderment, confusion; from bewilderment, loss of memory and of conscious self-control; from this perturbation or ruin of self-control comes the disappearance of intuitive understanding; and from this ruin of intuitive understanding comes the ruin of man himself."
>
> – Bhagavad Gita II - 62.63

In the Attempt of Reconnecting

The ideal of attaining self-realization and recovering lost knowledge had occupied the *Brahmins* for centuries. Much had been investigated, and the hundreds of scriptures are proof that no effort was spared to reach the one sole essence. But this aim would not be achieved, and many versions emerged as time went by.

The *Bhagavad Gita* summarizes the thought and basic disciplines of the complex religious tradition of this quest. Within a humanistic approach, the *Gita* emphasizes spiritual power as the means of overcoming obstacles and self-discipline as the foundation of its attainment. By means of knowledge and love, the *Gita* proposes sacrificing desire instead of the object and renouncing one's ego while living in the world. Happiness was believed to be achieved through a life based on righteousness and loving detachment.

There used to be real concern in maintaining the virtues of a *dharmic* life. However, the loss of soul-realization opened the mind to waste and imbalance. Duality and conflict remained as the tendency to decline continued.

The world drama now seemed "ready" for the paths we know as religions, as people still tried to refrain from negativity and still valued their positive potential. New actors came into being, some with prominent roles. Religious founders came onto the scene, bringing particular qualities.

They were instrumental in establishing communities and influenced ways of thinking in different places.

These souls also brought messages that created new ways of living and recovered social standards that were rapidly deteriorating. The main world religions were born with great power because there was genuine faith in their founders and first followers. Over time, the compilation of teachings into scripture and the formation of institutions were organized by disciples and followers. Methods and systems traveled far and wide, suffering translations and interpretations as the centuries went by.

India, in its turn, was to receive the first hordes of invaders, which would later dominate and deprive her of her treasures. While her ever-shrinking kingdoms were becoming hostile to one another, the subcontinent's frontiers were left open to attack by the Turks, Afghans, Persians, Greeks, and Moguls.

Castes

For a long time India was able to adjust to and often absorb the variety of people who settled on her soil. It was not uncommon for diametrically opposed religious and cultural groups to live very close to one another and yet manage to preserve their own worldviews.

The caste system definitely played a role in preserving traces of the ancient *Dharma,* because without its disciplines and traditions the land would have lost its connection with the past.

One thing has remained constant amid the invasions India has suffered: the *Brahmins* and their teachings. The *Brahmins* were responsible for trying to maintain the ideal of a noble culture, organizing a system of education and ethics that molded Indian civilization after the Fall.

The many *brahmanic* schools were the basis on which a spiritual and philosophical foundation was created. Their teachings gradually penetrated the four corners of the subcontinent, creating a link that would have been impossible to achieve by any secular authority. Even though the system was far from perfect, it managed to interconnect diverse creeds into a common pattern, maintaining the diversity of traditions, customs, and beliefs of many different peoples.

The social groups were initially divided into four castes, each possessing an ideal role: the *Brahmins*, to study and teach as well as preserve religion; the *Kshatriyas*, to administer and protect the country through temporal and military power; the *Vaishyas* or traders, to sustain the economic system through trade and charity; and the *Shudras,* to carry out the physical work. This system probably survived because of the autonomy and sense of community maintained by the groups within the structure.

One of the aspects that differentiated the castes was their understanding and view of life through the *gunas*. These were qualities or intrinsic "forces" considered to be found both in consciousness and in matter that influence desire, thought, and action.

The three codified qualities ranged from *sato*, the purest, through the medium quality, *rajo*, down to the lowest, *tamo*. The diversity of food was selected according to these, and even intentions and desires were evaluated in this context.

The castes were not a mere social class system but a complex arrangement of different groups living together, each possessing their own past as well as their own qualities and duties in society.

In time, the loss of core values and the dispersion of the different groups caused the meaning and responsibilities of the clans to disappear. The system eventually lost its significance and tended toward discrimination, prejudice, and exploitation.

At its best, this was a structure that tried to take innate tendencies into consideration in order to preserve them within social groups. Like other aspects of ancient Indian society, this system was based on the philosophy of a universal principle that was believed to be naturally responsible for the distribution of roles, responsibilities, and rights of every human being.

The Four Stages of Life

Enjoying life to its fullest was central to Indian culture. This idea also implied that upon reaching old age, all cravings for worldly things would have been satisfied. Desires could then be directed toward the spiritual adventure and the preparation of a new existence.

According to these principles, the first stage of human development comprised the period of growing up and education, called *Brahmacharya*. An exclusive characteristic of Indian culture was the master-disciple tradition, which was more than just a process of imparting and absorbing knowledge. The disciple dedicated his life to learning, often moving into his teacher's school, which was located in the teacher's home. More than a simple teacher, the *Guru* was expected to be a moral example and to embody his teachings. According to the disciple's capacity and vocation, the master would entrust him with all his techniques and secrets. It was a relationship that created skilled successors in art, philosophy, and science.

The time of maturity, *Grihastha*, meant the establishment and sustenance of a family and all pleasures and responsibilities related to it. The third stage started with the approach of old age. More than just renouncing work, retirement, or *Vanaprastha*, meant a gradual abandoning of an entire life, including family and possessions. The household could be entrusted to one's married children in case he wanted to move into a life of retreat and meditation.

The old traditions of India have always praised the ideal of *moksha* or *mukti*, a state of liberation from the inner bondage that causes suffering. In order to attain *mukti*, one made the effort to transcend the senses and remain identified with timeless reality. This stage of life was called *Sannyasa*, or renunciation, when the soul was focused on returning to a state of inner peace and contentment.

Creation is a mystery: Ko Veda?

At the beginning of the Copper Age there was a need to reflect and try to understand what had caused the Fall. Over time, this quest developed into efforts to prevent further losses.

Indian civilization was sustained by its own investigations, and many experiences and feelings from this period survived in the pages of her Vedas and scriptures. Her legacy was expressed through a set of beliefs related to the understanding of the soul's immortality and rebirth. This was a place that had created and sustained a complex polytheism based on a monotheistic principle in which all smaller deities are related to one God. In fact, there is probably no other region where the love for the Divine has been manifested with such depth and in such a variety of ways.

No other system had established its existence on such fascinating interpretations of life, and until the last century there had been no similar enterprise in trying to comprehend the movement of the human mind and the universe in its totality. India was once a sophisticated culture, where the ideal of perfection sought to combine in man the intellectual skills of the philosopher, the faith of the saint, and the aesthetic sense of the artist.

The desire to attain complete universal knowledge had generated a strong tendency toward assimilating other views rather than excluding them. This characteristic radically separates the ancient *Dharma* from other religions, which consider false all creeds but their own. In Hinduism, all creeds have some validity, as mentioned in the *Bhagavad Gita*:

> "...Whatever god someone adores, it is I who answer their invocation..."

The world population expanded and witnessed the ascension and fall of empires great and small. The multiplicity of languages and creeds as well as the geographical distance between people had enabled the development of deeply varied cultures. These differences, however, were increasingly becoming causes for incompatibility and discord. And confrontation had long since become part of the routine of kingdoms.

The human soul did not realize that it had lost the ideal of fighting its inner resistance. "Evil" was now to be found externally. Armies were created to fight "the enemy." The first battles were fought on the outskirts of cities; wars had a fixed time and place. After some time this rule was no longer observed; the enemy could be anywhere, anytime. The cities and their civil population, their women and children, were no longer respected. The decline of human character was vertiginous. There were no customs or systems that could stop the growing suffering.

Conscience, once free and creative, a space to experience peace and joy, no longer recognized itself. Self-awareness became limited to physical references. One was reduced to origin, gender, and status—to the color and religion into which the soul was born. One's original attributes were forgotten and the consciousness of being a soul gave way to the perishable identity of being "some" body.

Unfulfilled desires multiplied into negative tendencies. Vices became "habits"; violence was but a part. Everything was incorporated into the established moral. The *Dharma* was over.

Swadharma, the path of self-rule, inner harmony, and love, was no longer something worth following. Religions became "corporeal." They were embraced to the extent that they guaranteed credibility, or else they became a way of life. They were no longer the adopted means of having inner experiences; one was simply born into them. They came with the parents of the body and existed within the body of society. There were exceptions, but they were rare.

In fact, religion had inverted its role, becoming established ideology and making use of force to exercise power. Inquisitions persecuted and punished; plunderers hid their weapons behind the banners of indoctrination.

Everywhere massacres and conquests were happening behind the mask of religion, while conquerors enjoyed their achievements and "discoveries" of new lands. Power had never been so desired or exercised. The world entered the Iron Age.

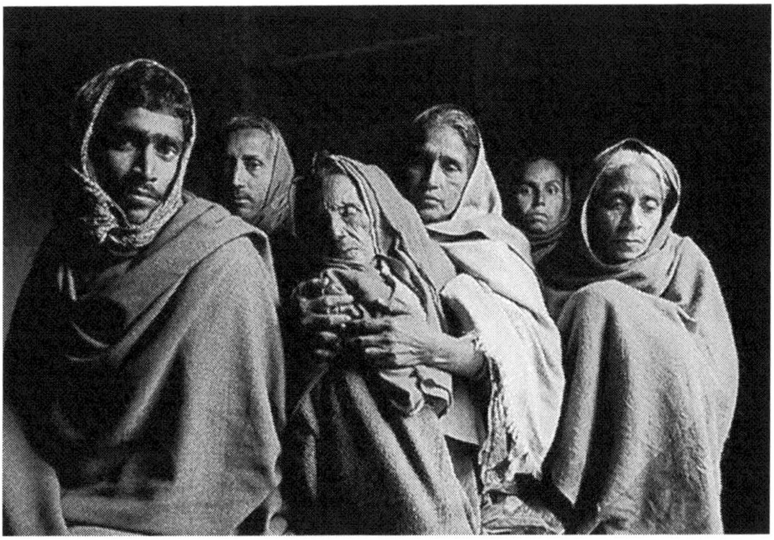

Kali Yuga

The last age is one of steep decay. As if alloy has been mixed into the soul, it has become hard to discern what is real. Lack of inner direction leaves the self at the mercy of fate, burdening the subconscious with frustrations and fears. There is hardly any respite.

Some say we live on the edge of history, for all systems, creeds, and ideologies seem to have played out their acts on this world stage.

Kali Yuga—the Age of Death—warns us that there is a single celestial degree left in the soul, and the light of the moon is no more to be seen.

There was a time when history was determined by human principles and cosmovisions, when the spirit compelled matter. As the ages went by, the wisdom we once possessed as a birthright was gradually replaced by the materialistic drive. It has been said that humankind is lost when the religious no longer have access to their inner nature, the poets no longer have access to their intuition, the intellectuals no longer have access to their love for truth, and the leaders no longer have access to their honesty and decision-making skill. Still, the eternal "drama" must go on.

Many subplots are now visible within one unique play, and despite the variety of circumstances and events, the basis of human life is essentially the same. Our spiritual condition continues to be the driving power of the wheel of history. Even in the depths of darkness all scenes are but a part of an unlimited plot. Life is a "play" with an order, where souls who have been playing a part since the beginning coexist with those who came after the Fall. Joining them later are many "new actors," souls that first descend from the subtle realm and continue to expand the global population.

India – the Night of Brahma

Few regions have witnessed so much aggression, dispute, and plunder; so many migrations and changes of government; and such a variety of religions, creeds, and customs as the Indian subcontinent. In the ancient land, empires and kingdoms have ascended and decayed, languages have been born and mixed into dialects, and nations have flourished and disappeared.

Deprived of her ancient treasures, with no clear knowledge of her origins, Mother India's many incarnations seem to have exhausted her. Undoubtedly, she still gives birth to great children, but their impact is too small in the face of her adversities. There is very little left of the wonders of ancient Bharat.

Swaraj, the ideal system of government based on self-rule, has become a myth. Illegality, corruption, and violence easily gained sway in a world shattered by decay and unconsciousness.

Liberation from British rule and the emergence of Mahatma Gandhi on the political scene brought new hopes in the last century. Gandhi revived the ideal of establishing *Ram Raj*, a society structured on human values and spiritual principles based on the memories of a long lost Golden Age. But the ideal that nurtured his dreams would never materialize.

Gandhi realized through his own experience that true liberation could not be achieved by mere conquest of power. He knew that inner transformation had to be achieved first. Thanks to his leadership and practice of non-violence, India ultimately gained its independence. However, he would soon witness the division of his own people due to political manipulation and religious discord.

"You, nescient, wandering throughout the world and searching for a myriad of imaginary gods. Have you not heard the many scriptures announcing that only God is knowledge?"

– *Subramania Bharati - Tamil Poet*

The Decline of Bhakti

India's soul has survived all kinds of difficulties, even if her early enthusiasm for spiritual exploration increasingly turned into unquestioned acceptance. But how could one possibly remember the origin of one's traditions after so long, the story behind those deities people continued to remember? There was certainly forgetfulness as well as a great deal of adulteration of the ancient knowledge—of the very essence that once made the land so great.

India's many scriptures, initially written in short verses, were mainly based on the experiences of *yogis* in deep contemplation. There was a need to understand and recover what had been lost. The Vedas, for example, can be read as a compendium of every aspect of life in the community of the period. It seems that for some reason those sages felt the need to retain every detail for posterity. There was certainly a fear of new calamities and the thought of saving important knowledge for future generations.

Over time, the addition of unreal plots deprived many texts of clarity and meaning. Many generations later, so much has been tested and tried, including the manipulation of negative energies.

Some *gurus* played a part in this by stimulating blind devotion. For a long time, spiritual guides were experienced teachers, living lives of simplicity and dedicating their time to meditation and supporting the community. Their relationship with the deities was based on the ideal of *Dharma*, the practice of kindness and cultivating spiritual qualities. The ancestors were personified goals, and *bhakti* was not the mere worship of images.

Even if a new breath of life was given to religion when Shankaracharya began his path of renunciation, Kali Yuga marks the end of the real spirit of search. The quest for truth could be discouraging, as quite a few *gurus* were not only claiming the title of *Bhagwan* but also letting people revere them as incarnations of God.

When *rishis* and *munis*—the sages and saints of ancient times—questioned reality or the nature of the Supreme, their answer was often "*neti, neti*"—"neither this, nor that." In the many discussions recorded in scriptures, the silence between the questions and the answers is evident. The truth those men were searching for was certainly beyond speech, and probably beyond their wisdom.

These were debates between "those whose hair was white and who, by having seen the children of their children and the duties of life accomplished had gone into the quietness and freedom of the forest." There, "in sessions of sweet and silent thoughts, all their sadness would disappear."

It is in Kali Yuga that spiritual crises deepen like karmic shadows, where misery, intolerance, violence, and corruption are omnipresent. Impoverishment of spirit can only be followed by material decline.

The world is on the edge; seekers no longer search for truth, and devotees can only cry out for support.

"We moderns are faced with the need of rediscovering the life of the spirit; we must experience it anew for ourselves. It is the only way in which to break the spell that binds us to the cycle of biological events. The wheel of history must not be turned back, and man's advance toward a spiritual life must not be denied...He must even be able to admit that the ego is sick for the very reason that it is cut off from the whole, and has lost its connection not only with mankind but with the spirit..."

– Freud and Psychoanalysis - C.G. Jung

Science

Waves of material development have transformed life in the course of the last two centuries. Facilities have become increasingly necessary for the comfort of the mind and body. Electricity, electronics, and atomic physics were the basis of a spectrum of inventions that placed scientists at the vanguard of history. Science also became indispensable to the government, where it sustains the production system, expresses the ideology of power, and defines the capacity for conquering and eliminating. The intellect of science rules.

The population has increased geometrically, concentrating in urban areas. Yet despite living so close together, man has never felt so alone. Science has become the foundation for the operation and sustenance of an overcrowded world and has succeeded in reducing labor for many. However, it has not been able to address or reduce serious problems. Together with technological advances, a number of serious difficulties emerged: pollution, climate change, a growing number of illnesses, scarcity of non-renewable resources, and the need to provide work, water, sanitation, and food to billions of people, just to mention a few. Both man and the earth have become increasingly ill.

The Science of the Psyche

> *"The contents of our consciousness manifest themselves in a highly complex form; the constellation of our thought, from the material contained in the memory, is almost totally unconscious. Therefore, we have to accept, whether it pleases us or not, something psychic, nonsentient, that up to the present, is a mere approximate concept."*
>
> *– Freud and Psychoanalysis - C.G. Jung*

In the West, the turn of the twentieth century has seen new attempts at rescuing the soul. When the deepest layers of the self were first observed, those who ventured into the inner journey realized how far they had diverged from their true nature and how fragile our life system had become. The relation between mental disorders and a separation from more subtle levels of being began to be established. The need to heal the soul was at the core of psychological investigations into the functioning of the mind and subconscious.

It didn't take long for those pioneers to realize that approaching the inner self is not an easy task. Their experiences have shown that the subconscious carries a variety of existences, a multiplicity of facets or personas that compose one's unique and personal history. These hidden traits have their own way of influencing and subtly dictating one's conscious choices. Fortunately some of these memories can be quite positive and can surface as newfound strength, self-respect, and other qualities.

The many schools that developed analytical approaches have managed to demonstrate, in one way or another, the incredible dynamics of the mental universe. They have also had to come to terms with their limits, as their methods were often deterministic and based on states of duality and conflict.

The transformative power of psychoanalysis has also been limited by its view of the nature of consciousness. Even when considered to be advancing into transcendental territory, the soul continued to be an unfathomable mystery to scientific investigations that could only create a theoretical basis to describe the soul's most visible manifestations. However, the birth of a new psychology seems to have cleared the limits of scientific logic and pointed toward an unlimited potential when referring to the spirit.

"It took an incredible decadence for man to accept materialistic theories such as those of Lamarck and Darwin. All traces of confidence in a divine order and harmony, and of legitimate pride, must have vanished in our lack of reaction against the science that lowers us to the brute state of so-called prehistoric man or anthropoid. Those who have steered humanity towards such stultification are mad men or criminals."

– Le Roi de la Theocratic Pharaonique - R. A. Schwaller de Lubicz

In Search of an Origin

Science still faces controversy when it comes to explaining the origin of man, and the debate between Darwin's theory of evolution and the old paradigm of creation by a Supreme Being continues. For many, this is a subject close to the heart, and it repeatedly comes up in religious and academic discussions with renewed passion and zeal.

We know that certain issues have never been able to be clarified by the divine creation theory, such as the nature of events prior to the Creator's will or the reason why a state of perfection would be subject to decline.

Evolutionism, on the other hand, is not able to approach issues related to the mind or to account for anomalies in its dating techniques. It has also never been able to locate the missing link that supposedly connects humans to simians, nor has it explained certain fossil records that have shaken its tenets. Besides, the model of a cosmos originating in a Big Bang completely ignores consciousness as the basis of life.

The ancient perspective of a cyclic universe brings out concepts that may fill in some of the gaps in our understanding of the processes of life on this planet.

In essence, this vision understands geology and biology, and the flora and fauna that belong to it, as dispersed results of great cataclysms that occur in every cycle. At its core is the subtle interconnectedness of life forms across time and space as well as changes and mutations happening in relatively short periods of time. The cyclic view is not related to any theory of creation, for in it the universe is seen as a complex structure of energy patterns that can neither be created nor destroyed.

The cycle is understood as a self-organized arrangement of repetition, an eternal continuum of time and space. Yet it also considers the participation of a highest form of consciousness whose role is to ignite and restore our spiritual vitality and strength. Creation is a cyclic process; it is a transformation triggered by a change in consciousness of a world of chaos and disorder into its original state of order.

"The Universe in its unmanifested form is conceived as the most minute point from which the expansion of the world takes place and into which, completing the cosmic cycle, it recedes."

— 'The Tantric Way' - Ajit Mookerjee and Madhu Khanna

As it entered the atomic dimension, scientific reasoning had to reorganize its paradigms more radically than ever. This brought science closer to concepts postulated by ancient civilizations, especially those in the East, where *yogis* visualized a multi-dimensional world in constant interaction and movement.

As parallels between old postulates and modern observations converge, a new breed of scientists is now making use of intuition and spiritual concepts. They know that the two approaches are complementary in the quest for a deeper understanding of the fundamental structure of life.

We've heard about experiments conducted on the subtle influence of thoughts and intentions on physical substances or energies. It has already been established that the mental state of an observer has a direct effect on the object observed and that consciousness exerts an invisible influence on matter.

> *"The transmutability of the elements has been shown in many ways. For example, it is possible, by bombarding certain elements with extremely rapidly-moving electrical particles, to change them into others, and to even produce elements which do not occur in nature because they are unstable (radioactive). We go even further. It is possible to produce matter, such as electrons, from radiation (light). Thus the ultimate constituent of the universe of the physicist is energy of radiation - that is, light.*
>
> *Thus the (ancient Hindu) Samkhya theory is in absolute agreement with the results of physics. The atomic theory is the product of the Western mind. In his naïve way the Western scientist generalizes the experience that one can subdivide matter until one meets an ultimate particle into an atomic theory assuming many elements. The Hindu philosopher goes much further and reduces everything to one element."*
>
> *– Joseph Kaplan quoted by Swami Prabhavananda - The Spiritual Heritage of India*

"The man who is captive in the structure of respectability, of repression, of imitation and adjustment -- this man is not living. Everything he does is a mere adjustment to some pattern."

– *Inner Transformation - Krishnamurti*

The System

The past century has seen the world population grow and multiply into billions. In order to feed and sustain this massive number of people, a new production pace had to be set. While on the economic front electronics replaced manufacturing, cultural and business patterns were easily spread through globalization.

However, this did not come packaged as the freedom of choice advertisers and pundits wanted us to buy, but in the form of highly priced commodities. Underneath most new trends is clear conformity to social dictates and a lifestyle devoid of deeper meaning. On behalf of respectability, we have increasingly become more "individualistic," protected by "rights" and guided by "responsibilities." The capacity of consumption demarcates our social movements and influences our attitudes. Even our idols have become trademarked products.

Still, life goes on, even when we find ourselves tired, with little capacity for compassion and cooperation. The age of information has certainly managed to bring the world closer, though it has not been able to create the so-called global village. Thanks to electronic devices and media, we are entertained and informed, yet the more our racing minds are occupied, the weaker our attention span, creativity and intellectual power become. As a result, we often react impulsively to circumstances rather than consciously acting on them.

Discerning can also become difficult with ethical boundaries that are so blurred. Contemplation used to be the means for reflecting and judging, but now there is a constant need to relate. We have come to fear rejection and loneliness; we lack mature references as well as real support.

Altruistic love, family support and loyal friendships are becoming as rare as basic moral principles and manners. Still, it is suggested that there has never been a time of so much respect for freedom and conquest of rights, even when nearly all systems have been replaced by a single ideology, whose foundation lies exclusively on the material knowledge of existence.

In the midst of it all, the soul survived — though with less control over its destiny, almost as a prisoner of its own limitations.

Held in the grip of fears and desires, enduring the demands of its will, the mind remains deprived. Despite material achievements, the spirit suffers.

"Man is now incredibly close to the greatest changes ever witnessed. To witness these changes with the safety of understanding means that we must question many of our accepted theories and be prepared to accept that which seems to provide greater clarity. The metaphysical — the consciousness of man — is about to be separated from its physical surroundings for a brief period of change and renewal. The man who identifies with and understands only the physical energies will experience ignorance and agony. Those who can step away will be observers and understanders of change, and will experience the heights of the civilization to follow."

– Earth in Bondage - Roger Dahlberg

The Mahabharat

All cosmogonies refer to a historical period of darkness, a time when humanity faced great challenges amid terrible calamities. These periods are said to be the consequences of man's ignorance, the results of his own deeds. At the same time, there seems to be a connection between these tribulations and man's redemption, as if the period of darkness was the condition for the resurgence of light.

In a cycle that has already witnessed moments of prosperity and fall, victory and defeat, we can expect a different turn at this crucial period at the end of Kali Yuga. The transition to a new cycle has been remembered in most scriptures and was also predicted in the great Indian epic of the Mahabharat:

> "Politics will be without principles, the laws without love and businesses without ethics; physical pleasures will be in its extreme; there won't be respect for seniors, no love for children; science will be used for the destruction of humanity; irreligion will go under the name of religion; bhakti will be filled with blind faith and devotion; edible items will be sold in small packets and milk in bottles; the clans will have lost their responsibilities and there won't be purity between the members of the same family; man will eat man (cannibalism); untimely death will result in wandering spirits; the weather and the seasons will be unpredictable."

Prophets and seers from different places and times have visualized and commented on what the world would face before transformation. The Bible, the Koran, and the Talmud contain detailed descriptions of signs and omens related to this time.

The book of the Apocalypse cautions: *"the one who has led to captivity, will be led captive; the one who has killed by the sword will be killed by the sword,"* (13:10) defining the final period as a *karmic* settlement. The medieval seer Michel de Nostradamus dedicated a number of his centuries to a description of what he called "*a revolution that will change all notions of time,*" when "*divine word will be given to matter, and heaven and earth will comprehend occult and mystical events.*" Pests, famine, wars, and earthquakes are quoted in all prophecies.

In our own time, as political utopias come to an end and a new order has not yet been established, new prophecies are arising:

> *"It is already obvious that the annihilation of conflict in the systems of the post-war age, despite all the Nobel peace prizes given to a variety of different chiefs of the losers with the good will of political intermediaries, won't bring the "eternal Kantian peace" but, most probably, exactly the opposite. The unique world, finally realized and recognized as such, but still condemned to the fetishist form and attacked by the commodities system crisis; it reveals itself as a vision of terror, of a coming world civil war—a war in which there won't be firm fronts, only outbursts of blind violence coming from all levels.*
>
> *The game of the world market, which has absorbed and assimilated all other forms, does not allow losers to go home quietly anymore; it is successively destroying all the possibilities of a dignified existence. When these men, people, regions and states realize that they will never have a chance to win and that inevitable future defeats will deprive them of any possibility of living, they will throw the chessboard*

> on the floor and discard all the rules of the so-called world civilization. These democratic rules of the bourgeois and enlightened "worldly reason" are, in essence, abstract and insensitive, generating a movement that gives birth to its destructive laws and executes them mechanically until the terrible end..."
>
> — *The Collapse of Modernization* - Robert Kurz

The "End of Times" has been feared for centuries, even more so when wars and transitions inspired proximity to the prophecies. Still, humanity has never had so many reasons to feel close to the end of an era. One doesn't need to be a prophet to see a course of destruction, a process triggered by our lack of awareness and respect. Famine, terrorism, social injustice, civil war, environmental destruction, and the nuclear threat have become the specters of fear.

> "I see that the age we live in now is an age in which the whole evolution and impulse of consciousness has been deeper and deeper into matter, and therefore all the values that go with matter: wealth, power, ownership. I believe the clue to history is to realize that consciousness and the evolution of things are interdependent. And the clue to the actual evolving of consciousness is this: that through the years, the immortal spiritual being has gradually been stepping down into an ever closer identification with the body."
>
> — *The Spirit of the New Age* - Sir George Trevelyan

For some people, widespread loss of values and coherence has triggered a need for inner work and self-transformation. They know that change must begin from within. Only from a state of inner awareness can we realize how far we've gone in our infringement of the laws that rule the universe and govern our own existence.

Experiencing this as a reality and understanding how far we have moved away from it is something realized by only a few. However, at any given time it has always been only a small handful that has dared to live up to the challenges that determine the turns of history. These people were often misjudged and have seldom been recognized in their own time.

The world is again looking forward to lost integrity and benevolence. Far more than small-scale change or reform, it is the very foundation of life that needs to be recreated. And creating values is like creating religion: it must come from within, from the depths of the self, for only inner truth has the power to transform.

"By death, the soul does not lose that which it has previously acquired. The experiences that man has done in past lives become instincts and push him towards progress, even if unconsciously. Even he who only wanted to know yoga will recover this desire. A yogi is one who searches for truth and who, by trusting in absolute justice, always does the best he can. He is superior to ascetics or to men of knowledge, and even greater than those who perform action with some motive. Therefore, be a yogi, O Arjuna!"

– Bhagavad Gita VI - 44, 46

Arjuna

The famous epic of Mahabharat is about a period of transition and facing the inevitable, a time when two opposing clans can find no way to solve their disputes except by going to war. The battle devastates the world and leaves only a few survivors.

The plot centers on the fight of the "awakened" heroes and their adventures before the end of a cosmic cycle. Its core chapters, known as the Bhagavad Gita, graphically describe the doubts and despair of the mythic hero Arjuna and his brothers when confronting their adversaries.

Standing on the battlefield, Arjuna suddenly realizes that his enemies are his own relatives and friends, leading a far greater army. The vision of his uncles, cousins, and teachers on the opposing side made him consider giving up the fight. However, his guide advises him to let go of his fear and attachment, and after realizing the invisible roots of the situation he feels able to move ahead.

Arjuna's dilemma gradually disappears as he comes to understand the intricacies of spiritual reality and the reasons why his actions could make a difference. His anguish and need for clarity are expressed in a beautiful dialogue that could well take place between God and the human soul. It is a conversation that also exposes the inner challenges and trials of those who are willing to face and conquer their own weaknesses.

This story left deep roots in the ancient Indian psyche. *Ajna Chakra*—the center of energy located between the eyebrows—has remained as a memorial and indicator of awakening to higher consciousness.

* * *

*One whose happiness is within,
who is active within,
who rejoices within
and is illumined within
is actually the perfect mystic.*

– Bhagavad Gita, IV-7

The Need for Silence

It is well known that a peaceful mind can only develop out of deep inner stillness, out of silence that is not empty yet is absent of conflicts and fears. It is in a state of introspection that the soul finds the space to be heard and acknowledged and may become an observer of its own self. Love of solitude allows the mechanism of thinking to slow down and the needs of the mind to be recognized and nurtured. Our true potential can then gradually be realized.

Most of us are strangers to inner silence. We have never learned how to experience it, and have instead kept busy through activities and constant external demands. Our society has its highs in consumerism, where wasteful practices continue to feed the vicious cycle while the vast majority strives simply to survive.

The prevailing lack of altruistic love seems connected to our loss of self-esteem and our difficulty in experiencing inner fulfillment. Relationships may be unconsciously used to meet these needs, reducing the possibility of true and longstanding connections. The impossibility of deep change has forced us to rely on references and trends that have been masking our lack of inner strength.

The increasing importance assigned to physical appearance and status symbols has deprived us of a more subtle level of communication—of being comfortable in silence, of looking people in the eyes and appreciating their qualities. Even our myths have lost their supportive role. In an imperceptible movement, wisdom has been drawn into the artifices of ego, decreasing the value of a wise intellect.

But still there is silence. The sweet stillness that is able to regenerate the mind and connect it to the Source. As the meeting of hearts take place, our deepest needs are fulfilled. The soul gains strength, a power that irradiates and influences even the tiniest bits of matter.

This silence lies in the deepest layers of our memory, but it is an external frequency that awakens it, as a subtle signal invoking one's attention. It is a soundless chant, a subtle wave that reaches us from beyond.

By connecting with the Divine, the soul receives a love that is unlimited, a bliss that is its birthright. It is the beginning of a journey through an ocean of inner experiences toward the destiny of completion. We listen to this signal by merging with the loving frequency of God's mind.

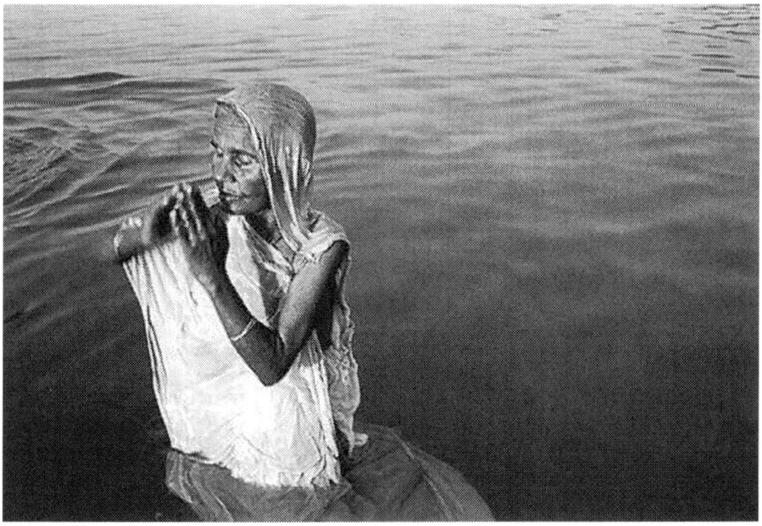

*Where do you stand behind them all,
my lover, hiding yourself in the shadows?
They push you and pass you by
on the dusty road, taking you for nothing.
I wait here weary hours spreading
my offerings for you, while passers-by
come and take my flowers, one by one,
and my basket is nearly empty.
The morning time is past, and the noon.
In the shade of evening my eyes are
drowsy with sleep. Men going home
glance at me and smile and fill me
with shame. I sit like a beggar maid,
drawing my skirt over my face, and
when they ask me, what it is I want,
I drop my eyes and answer them not.
Oh, how, indeed, could I tell them
that for you I wait, and that you
has promised to come....*

– Gitanjali - XLI Rabindranath Tagore

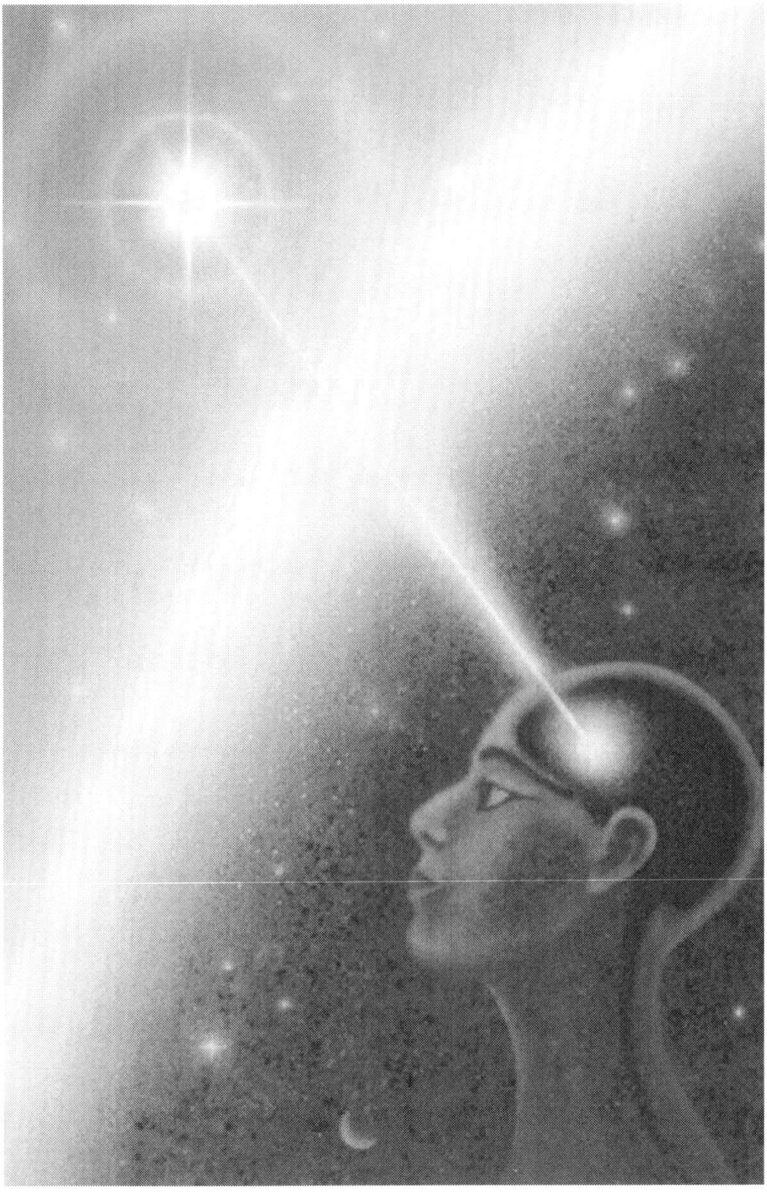

Sangam Yuga

Incognito as the seed that nurtures the potential tree, the invisible seed of consciousness is first planted and then carefully grown. When the fruits ripen, the earth is again filled with vitality and wisdom.

Sangam is the confluence of rivers with the Ocean — God and his creation. It has been portrayed as a divine dance, in which every movement is a purifying alchemy and spiritual experiences are meant to transform a mind of iron into a mine of gold.

As the end of each night unfolds into a new day and the last sighs of the winter bring the fresh air of spring, it's in the darkest hour that the seeds of enlightenment are eternally sown.

There is a perspective we can get only from outer space, where our planet stands out as a sparkling pearl surrounded by unlimited sky. A cosmic arrangement of planets and stars gravitate in a continuous movement, in absolute synchrony. We can see this as a floating world, a giant vessel built for navigation.

Beyond this universe there is a vision: an "eye" that has the power to focus on anything it chooses. Merged with this vision is a story — the knowledge of three existing energies operating in the universe; eternal realities similar only in their nature.

The forms of both the soul and the fundamental elements that make up matter are those of tiny particles of light, points of infinitesimal dimension.

However, there is a fundamental difference between them, and this difference defines the limits between the physical and the metaphysical. The tiny dots that make up the field that sustains and permeates everything are, in essence, light—a light that is not conscious. While subatomic particles may have properties and patterns—their own *sanskaras* of sorts—they are not self-aware nor do they have intellect or mind.

Even though this energy field may react, store, and propagate information, there is no thinking in the most subtle level of matter. Consciousness pertains to the soul alone and is the basis of human life.

We souls have been consciously playing out our roles as different characters, using different costumes and languages in a cycle of birth and rebirth. It is the soul that has been interacting with the world of non-conscious elements, living at different periods of time, and expressing and absorbing different habits and tendencies while maintaining a core personality.

The play goes on as changes continue to take place. Our inner truth and strength gradually fades, even while we find ways to minimize the loss. Journeying through time means we've ended up forgetting who we are, and we no longer recognize our spiritual identity.

This is the story of the human soul within the cycle of life, where the state of our world has always reflected the condition of our inner selves.

Yet there is still a third reality: a being of wisdom who remains beyond, a Soul that has never been subjected to reversals of time and fortune. He has kept the understanding, remained constant, and never entered the cycle of life and death.

There is a vision that doesn't need the eye to recognize, not even to be physically present to realize. His mind operates on another level, resides in another dimension, and is filled with accurate knowledge of the processes of the universe.

This third force or conscious energy is peculiar to One alone—the One who men for so long and in a myriad of ways have agreed to call "God."

The Divine Play

In ancient India, the boatman used to ask "*Kah paragah?*" or "Who is going to the other shore?" This is the origin of the word *Tirthankara*, an attribute of "those who crossed" the shores of time.

Sangam Yuga is a confluence bridging two very distinct and contrasting moments. It is as if on one shore one sees the shadows of a dying system, and on the other the gradual formation of a new order. This age exists as a state of awareness because the movements of the world are still propelled by the old forms and will continue to be until before collapsing.

The transition from Kali Yuga into a new Sat Yuga begins with the awakening of the spirit. It is the blossoming of truth in thought and action together with sustained efforts over a period of time that allows us to recognize the hidden aspects of life.

What we call "creation" is certainly not a mere variation of structures. New ideologies and social systems have always introduced some reform but have never been able to generate great change.

Within a cosmic cycle, the Confluence Age is the period for perfecting the soul. It is when the understanding of destiny and free will along with the observation of spiritual principles once again become part of the play. It is at this time that the old saying "*hum so, so hum*"—that which I was, I shall be again—is given meaning as we begin to consciously create our destiny.

This knowledge is amplified by the recognition of an all-penetrating order, an arrangement that interconnects what seems loose, weaving an invisible fabric and "putting right" what has gone wrong.

Whether we realize it or not, we are influenced by the movements of *karmic* laws. Nothing is unchanging, nothing remains isolated. We humans are integrated into a universe in constant motion.

It is due to the existence of a predestined karmic "plan" that one person's actions are linked up with someone else's experience. We can call it nature, destiny, or fate. This unseen force is the basis of the interplay between souls. Everything moves according to the plan of the "drama."

This pattern also applies to the reacting forces of nature, whose elements possess an inherent power to respond. For this reason the end of Kali Yuga has been remembered as a time of destruction and renewal brought about by calamities both natural and manmade.

The secret, then, is to know the plan, to have a map of the changes and take part in them. A new creation does not emerge out of the blue or from simple wishful thinking. A power is needed: someone to inspire, influence, and in some way determine those actions that will bring about not only personal improvement but collective change as well.

We also need the power of truth: someone who can touch our hearts and minds, which have for so long been conditioned by ego messages. In deep darkness we need to see the light of a mind that is not struggling with fear or uncertainty. We need support, clarity, and loving guidance: someone who knows us deeply and is aware of our potential future.

Prahbu Ki Lila—the ancient perspective of cyclic renewal —considers this third acting force, best translated as "the drama in which God also plays a role."

"Your call goes towards Hindus, Buddhists, Sikhs, Jains, Parsis, Muslims and Christians. They all come, gather around Your throne and thread a garland of love in adoration of You...."

– Bharata Bhagya Vidhata –
The Bestower of Fortune of Bharat
Rabindranath Tagore

Shiva Nataraja

One of the most accurate memorials of the Confluence Age is that of God in the symbolic posture of *Nataraja*—the King of Dancers—his dance being the representation of the supreme energy in movement.

Shiva dances over *Apasmara Purusha*, the demon that represents human arrogance, implying that humility is the virtue through which man can begin to reach a level of spiritual perception. On the one hand, he holds a deer, the fluctuating mind of man that must be controlled; in another, he shakes a drum, the symbol of creative energy. In his third hand he holds a flame — the image of destruction; his fourth hand, in the posture of *abhaya mudra,* says: 'Do not be afraid, as I destroy, I also protect'.

The circle of fire surrounding him symbolizes the eternal and constant movement of the universe in the age of Creation (at the confluence of the cycle), preservation (during the Golden and Silver Ages) and destruction (at the end of the Iron Age).

Out of the many symbols, the most significant seems to be the least noticed. The dot on his forehead—his "third eye"—representing the invisible and incorporeal form of the Supreme Soul. It also reveals that his thoughts are never related to the material world, for his vision is of a spiritual nature.

Shiva is also known as the *Lord of Yoga* and the teacher of an art that has long disappeared. Raja Yoga is a spiritual practice — a subtle union with the Highest Soul, remembered as a Being of Light by mystics of all times.

These experiences leave eternal impressions on the soul. The yogi experiences a relationship with the Divine through meditation. This direct connection empowers the mind and gives clarity to the intellect, allowing the soul to release the burdens and sorrows of its past.

Shiva Nataraja is no longer just a powerful metaphor. Those who experience the challenges of this time realize that receiving Divine support is the basis for self-transformation and the beginning of a new cycle.

* * *

*'Leave your throne in the sky
and come down to earth'*

— Indian devotional song

There are memorials related to divine intervention in all cultures of the planet. Their archetypes may vary, but they have been present in the minds of all people, in a very special way, since early times.

We may have distanced ourselves from signs and feelings of the spirit, but our innermost mind seems to have preserved a record of experiences common to every human soul. The mechanism of our subconscious only manifests something as a desire once it has been previously experienced. Similarly, each movement of the spirit through history can be seen as an attempt to bring back the qualities humanity once possessed and has now lost.

Most of the symbols, rituals, and festivals of India are memorials of a period of transition, when a new cycle is born. They point to the most auspicious time, when the Creator himself has to reenact his own special role.

In India, ancient songs are still passionately sung calling for *Patitpavana*, "the Purifier," and the Bestower of Knowledge and Happiness to come and teach the right methods for liberating the soul from sorrow.

Coming across millions of such devoted people can be a striking experience. The way India was able to preserve millenary traditions and continue with the same practices today is absolutely amazing. Even in the understanding of time, the word *kal* can still be used to indicate yesterday, today, or tomorrow. This firm idea of recurrence is also seen in a beautiful passage of the Gita:

> *"Whenever the Sacred Law fails, and evil rises its head, I return to re-establish the true Dharma..."*
>
> *– Bhagavad Gita IV - 7*

Ancient Raja Yoga

"There, where there is no darkness, nor night, nor day, nor nonbeing, there is the Auspicious One alone, absolute and eternal. There is the glorious splendor of that light, from whom, in the beginning sprang ancient wisdom."

– Svetasvatara Upanishad - IV,18

In ancient times, the quest for deep understanding and realization was based on inner experience. Because spiritual perception was at the foundation of the highest thoughts, a subject as fluid as time could be approached in all its subtleties. The state of transcendence, often combined with empirical observation, was able to produce extraordinary views. The cyclic perspective not only considered eternity but also tried to understand the physical and ethical implications inherent in unending life.

Sacred symbols related to this peculiar vision of history were engraved on ancient tombs and temples. This was done in a time when ancient mystical sciences were raising the same questions as today's higher mathematics and quantum physics. The attainment of higher knowledge was then believed to be intrinsic to spiritual revelation.

The nostalgic and idealistic philosophy of ancient India once thoroughly pursued the truth about the *Kalachakra* — the cosmic cycle of time. It also left behind legends about people who once knew the secrets of the past and future — the *Chakravartins,* or spinners of the wheel.

One of their secrets was that when it comes to things of the spirit, understanding goes hand in hand with self-transformation. Only then can knowledge become wisdom, a real source of strength.

Today we can once again "put the sacred wheel into movement" as we learn about past *yugas* and the crucial period we live in.

This is the age of creation, when we attain victory over our limitations and negativities. As we understand the secrets and move forward, we come to realize how *Dharnat Dharmah* — the law that nurtures and sustains the world — is once again being re-established.

Waves of Change

We live in a period of rapid transformation, when the need for a shift in consciousness and the reviewing of old paradigms are becoming acknowledged. Science, psychology, spirituality, and economic development are part of this dynamic. Holism is rescuing ancient concepts by considering humankind and nature in their entirety, while environmental awareness is inspiring sustainable development.

The rational, mechanistic thought that has for so long defined the scientific approach is beginning to consider intuition and the subjective aspects of life. The old analytical posture searches for synthesis; the linear view considers the cyclic. Feminine attributes such as spirituality, tolerance, and courage are being recognized once again.

Ethics and transparency are being emphasized together with a replacement of old attitudes; competition is giving way to cooperation, quantity leaving space for quality, domination seeking participation.

The shift away from personal interests to values and feelings that belong to the spirit suggests not only that the old formula has failed but that there has been a change in self-identity.

Previously, the fear of losing prestige and position fed the competitive system in a hierarchic structure; now a number of administrators and strategists seek to take understanding, empathy, and mutual support into account. These changes are still small-scale, but they are significant in their approach because they encompass almost every area of human activity. They show that something is emerging from the individual and transforming into the collective.

A growing interest in spiritual matters and, in particular, the legacy of ancient traditions is also part of this movement. If a few decades ago blind faith and unquestioned submission gave rise to "the death of God," today people speak of a return to the Divine.

It has become impossible to deny that our souls need to experience the clarity, peace, and love that belong to their innermost nature.

This love for truth existed in the ancient world, and this short narrative was possible because of its surviving heritage and present revival. The cyclic perspective can, in fact, be considered the ancient *Dharma*'s origin, gradual decline, and final recurrence.

But there is more. A spiritual renaissance—unique and still incognito—is taking form in the minds of people all over.

However, it is almost impossible in the limited space of a short essay to outline a perspective that is many million times greater. This is a fascinating story that will always defy words and writing. A great deal has also been left out, because a deeper approach definitely belongs to a posterior stage of knowledge requiring meditative experience. As the Indian saying goes, "Even if the oceans turned into ink and all trees into paper, even then, History could never ever be written."

In any case, the essence can be the tip of the iceberg, as it can be the catalyst that awakens interest. At the moment spiritual truth touches our being, a new dimension is discovered and things seem to be willing to reveal their inner meaning. We begin to read the signs of this play of life.

As actors and spectators of this unlimited cosmic drama, we are sure to be nearing a "grand finale." The time will come when spiritual reality will not be visible and experienced only by a few, but by everyone.

In India, *Gyan* is the word for spiritual knowledge, *Vigyan* for science. There will come a time when that which works in silence will reveal something to the mind's eye. It won't then take long for a series of events to unfold and usher in a new era.

Everything new begins in the invisible.

Bibliography

1. "Der Wille zur Macht "
The Will to Power – Eternal Recurrence
by Friedrich Nietzsche – translated by T.N. Foulis, London 1910

2. "Zur Umerziehung des deutschen Volkes"
On the Re-education of the Germans
by Carl Jung
In Basler Nachrichten, nr. 486, 1946

3. Bhagavad Gita II – 20, 22, 23
translated by Swami Vireswarananda
Shri Ramakrishna Math, Madras

4. The First Principles
by Origen Adamantius – translated by G.W. Butterworth
Society of Promoting Christian Knowledge, London, 1936

5. Bhagavad Gita III - 4, 5, 20
translated by Shri Purohit Swami
Faber and Faber Limited, London

6. The Dream of a Ridiculous Man
by Fyodor Dostoevsky
Lindsay Drummond Limited, London, 1945

7. Metamorphoses – Book One
by Ovid (Publius Ovidius Naso) – translation by A.E. Watts
University of Berkeley CA, 1954

8. Myths of China and Japan
by Donald A. Mackenzie
Gresham Publishing Co., London, 1923

9. Genesis II:8;I:26,27
The New English Bible, Penguin Books 1974

10. Mahabharat – Shanti Parva Mokshadharma, 231
Indian Myth and Legend – translated by Donald A. Mackenzie
Gresham Publishing Co., London

11. The Eternal World Drama
BK Jagdish Chander Hassija
Om Shanti Press, India, 1985

12. Ibid.

13. Olympia
by Anthea Church
Published by Confluence magazine, Hong Kong, 1986

14. Metamorphoses – Book One
by Ovid (Publius Ovidius Naso)
University Tutorial Press Ltd., London, 1931

15. The Forgotten Books of Eden
From the Portuguese edition "Apócrifos – Os Proscritos da Bíblia"
cap VIII:2, compiled by Maria Helena de Oliveira Tricca
Editora Mercuryo, São Paulo, 1991

16. Timaeus
by Plato – translated by H.D.P. Lee
Penguin Books, London, 1965

17. Ibid. The New English Bible
Penguin Books, 1974

18. Ibid. The Forgotten Books of Eden

19. Maitri Upanishad 4
translated from the Sanskrit by Robert Ernest Hume
Oxford India Paperbacks

20. Ibid. Genesis 10:32;11:1,2

21. Ibid. Genesis IV.2

22. The Epic of Gilgamesh
Penguin Books, London, 1960

23. Ibid. Genesis V.4

24. In the Beginning
Immanuel Velikovsky
at the Velikovsky Archive

25. The Hindu Scriptures - Introduction
by Rabindranath Tagore — transalted by N. MacNicol and others,
Everyman London, 1938

26. Rig Veda X, 129
from "The Wonder that was India"
A.L. Basham, Rupa & Co. Calcutta, 1963

27. Svetasvatara Upanishad VI, 1
from "The Wonder that was India" Ibid.

28. Katha Upanishad — First Adhyaya
Vishnudharmottan on the arts, APA Publications, India

29. Brihadaranyaka Upanishad
Hinduism Today, Madras, India

30. Pattuppattu, Tirumuruganarrupadai 285-90
from "The Wonder that was India" Ibid.

31. Rasa
Mandakini Trivedi
Article published by The Times of India

32. Fa-Hsien
from "The Wonder that was India" Ibid.

33. Bhagavad Gita II - 62.63
Philosophies of India
by Heinrich Zimmer

34. Subramania Bharati, Tamil Poet
Unesco magazine, Portuguese edition

35. Freud and Psychoanalysis
by C.G. Jung
Routledge & Kegan Paul, London, 1961/Vol 4

36. "Ich liebe meines Wesens Dunkelstunden"
I love the dark hours of my being, from Love Poems to God
by Rainer Maria Rilke

37. Freud and Psychoanalysis
by C.G. Jung — Ibid.

38. Le Roi de la Theocratic Pharaonique
by R. A. Scwhaller De Lubicz
Flammarion, Paris, 1961

39. Physics and Philosophy
by Werner Heisenberg
Harper & Row, New York, 1962

40. Joseph Kaplan quoted
by Swami Prabhavananda
The Spiritual Heritage of India, Vedanta Society of California

41. Inner Transformation
by Jiddu Krishnamurti
Portuguese edition, Editora Cultrix, São Paulo, 1977

42. Earth in Bondage
by Roger Dahlberg - Ibid.

43. The Collapse of Modernization
by Robert Kurz
Portuguese edition, Editora Paz e Terra, São Paulo, 1992

44.The Spirit of the New Age
by Sir George Trevelyan
London, 1984

45. Bhagavad Gita VI - 44,46 - Ibid.

46. Bhagavad Gita IV-7 - Ibid.

47. Gitanjali - XLI
by Rabindranath Tagore
Macmillan India Limited, 1981

48. Bharata Bhagya Vidhata – The Donor of Fortune of Bharat
by Rabindranath Tagore

49. Bhagavad Gita IV-7 Ibid.

50. Svetasvatara Upanishad - IV, 18
Krishna Yajur Veda, Hinduism Today

Photo & Images Credits

Solar cross on the front page – author unknown

1. Swastika wall detail – photo by Simone Boger
2. 'Neheh' -- Egyptian hieroglyph for the cyclical nature of time
3. Original artwork by Marie Binder
4. Nath Charit by Bulaki -- Jodhpur, India 1823
5. Cosmos – Fractal art by Vicky Brago-Mitchell
6. Garden image – artist unknown
7. Vishnu – artist unknown
8. Rasa Lila – artist unknown
9. Temple Moonrise -- Shri Swaminarayan Mandir Atlanta, USA -- photo by JLMPhoto
10. Sita Ram – artist unknown
11. Devi – photo by Swami Premgit
12. 'The Golden Mountain' from India Pictorial and Descriptive by William Henry Davenport Adams -- London 1888
13. Radha Krishna – artist unknown
14. Durga – artist unknown
15. Young brahmins – artist unknown
16. "India" – photo by Marcelo Buainain
17. Bindu – Gouache on paper – Rajasthan c. 18th century from 'The Tantric Way' by Ajit Mookerjee and Madhu Khanna
18. Arjuna – photo by Simone Boger
19. Battle of Tarain – artist unknown
20. "India" – photo by Marcelo Buainain
21. Raja Yoga – image by Brahma Kumaris
22. Shiva Nataraja – author unknown
23. Supreme Soul Shiva – image by Brahma Kumaris
24. Flower of Life – author unknown

I apologize if I'm using your photo or artwork without acknowledging authorship. I tried my best to track all authors and get their permissions, but have not been able to source a few images. Do let me know if this applies to your work.

SIMONE BOGER is a Brazilian freelance journalist and writer who began her spiritual journey in her early twenties. Growing up in different places and living in foreign countries was the basis of her education. She spent many years in India covering news, exploring ancient knowledge and deepening her meditation practice.

She has been researching the links between ancient history and spirituality for over 30 years. As a longtime Raja Yoga practitioner she teaches and lectures on a variety of subjects related to spiritual knowledge and meditation. Her most recent book is called *The Power of Love – Returning to the Source*. More information as well as the digital version of this book is on her website at www.cycleoftime.com

Made in the USA
Charleston, SC
29 August 2014